To

MY WIFE REKHA

Contents

Preface

The Protection of Women from Domestic Violence Act, 2005 has been enacted by the Parliament with the objective of providing more effective protection of the rights of women guaranteed under the Constitution, who are victims of violence of any kind occurring within the family. The Act provides various civil reliefs to the victims of domestic violence in form of protection orders, residence orders, monetary reliefs, custody orders, compensation orders etc. The focus of the Act is on protection and rehabilitation of the victims of domestic violence.

Although reliefs provided under the Act are civil in nature, criminal procedure has been adopted under the Act for faster and effective handling of incidents of domestic violence.

One of important feature of the Act is recognition of the role of non-governmental orgnisations in fighting evil of domestic violence. Non-governmental orgnisations can be registered as service providers under the Act and can provide various services like shelter, counselling, medical aid to the victims of domestic violence.

The Act creates position of Protection Officer, who acts as a bridge between the Magistrate, aggrieved person, service provider, police etc. The Protection Officer discharges various critical functions including assisting the aggrieved person in filing Application before the Magistrate, preparing Domestic Incident Report, etc.

Domestic violence has been defined comprehensively under the Act. Domestic violence includes verbal abuse , emotional abuse, physical abuse, sexual abuse and economic abuse.

I am overjoyed to present the first edition of this book. The book has been written in form of section wise commentary. Relevant judgments of the Supreme Court and various High Courts have been incorporated at appropriate places. I hope readers will find this book useful.

Prologue

Women and men are born equal. The Constitution has granted equal rights to women. Women have every right to enjoy their political, social, cultural and economic rights which have been guaranteed by the Indian Constitution.

Unfortunately women have faced discrimination due to various historical, social and cultural factors. Domestic violence is one of outcomes of such discrimination. Women face incidents of domestic violence at their parental homes as well as at their matrimonial homes. Instances of domestic violence have remained largely invisible to society as domestic violence is perpetrated within four walls of home by a family member. Only few instances of domestic violence are reported in public domain.

Women are reluctant to report domestic violence to police, court and other public authorities on account of various reasons. There is perception among the victims that domestic violence is private matter and if such matter is made public, it will bring disrepute to the family. There is also social pressure for not reporting domestic violence incidents to police, court and other public authorities. Although there has been overall economic empowerment of women, as yet majority of women are economically dependent on family members for their livelihood. They are afraid that if they complain about domestic violence their survival may be stake. There is also lack of legal literacy among women and many of them are not aware of their rights and remedies available under various legislations. Further, women do not report domestic violence cases because approach of police, court and other public authorities is often insensitive, mechanical and critical. They are not sufficiently sensitive and proactive to handle domestic violence cases.

Women had enjoyed greater freedoms and rights in ancient India during vedic period. They had rights to participate in meeting and present their ideas and opinions. They had freedom to choose their husbands. They had rights to educate themselves and contribute to knowledge. In fact, there were many women who had attained high intellectual status and had contributed to contemporary civilization. Ghosa, Lopamudra, Maitreyi and Gargi were few of them. The ten hymns of Rig Veda are accredited to Maitreyi. The Rig Veda has long intellectual conversations between the sage Agasthya and his wife Lopamudra. Gargi composed several hymns that question the origin of all existence. Importance of women in ancient society can be inferred from the fact that many of ancient warriors were known by the name of their mother. For example, Arjun was also known as Kaunteya, which means son of Kunti.

The status of women gradually deteriorated due to various social, economic and cultural factors. As society became sedentary and agriculture became main occupation in society, patriarchal values became prominent and dominant. As time passed, various harmful customs like sati pratha, child marriage etc. emerged in the Indian Society. Some initiatives were taken during the colonial period for betterment of status of women. Sati Pratha was abolished vide Bengal Suttee Regulation 1829. Age of consent for sexual intercourse for all girls, whether married or unmarried, was increased vide Age of Consent Act, 1891. Child Marriage Restraint Act, 1929 was passed which fixed minimum age for marriage for girls and boys. Efforts were made by social reformers like Raja Ram Mohan Roy, Ishwar Chandra Vidya Sagar, Periyar T.Y.Ramasamy, Pandita Ramabai etc. for betterment of status of women. Mass movements of Mahatma Gandhi were great strides in emancipation and empowerment of women.

Indian independence was another milestone in emancipation and empowerment of women. Indian Constitution does not discriminate between men and women and grants equal rights to both of them. Article 15(3) empowered state to make special provisions for women, as women were at a disadvantageous position in comparison to men due to historical, social and cultural factors.

After independence, various steps were taken for empowerment of women. The suppression of Immoral Traffic in Women and Girls Act was enacted in 1956. The same was amended to include male and female who are exploited sexually for commercial purpose and renamed as Immoral Traffic (Prevention) Act, 1956. Commission of Sati Prevention Act was enacted in 1987 with the objective of prevention of practice of Sati and any activities which led to its glorification and its abetment. Dowry system has become deeply rooted in Indian Society. Women were facing frequent dowry related violence. Dowry Prohibition Act was enacted in 1961 to prevent giving or taking of dowry. Section 125 of Code of Criminal Procedure, 1973 provides for, *inter alia*, maintenance to married women. Indian Penal Code, 1860 was amended and Section 498 A was inserted therein vide Criminal Law (Second) Amendment Act, 1983 to protect women from cruelties inflicted by husband and his relatives. Section 304B was also inserted in the Indian Penal Code, 1860 vide Dowry Prohibition (Amendment) Act, 1986 to prevent increasing instances of dowry deaths in Indian Society. Indecent Representation of Women (Prohibition) Act, 1987 was passed with the objective to prohibit indecent representation of women through advertisements, or in publications, writings, paintings, figures or in any other manner.

Aforesaid initiatives were not sufficient for protection of women from incidences of domestic violence. Section 498A and Section 304B of the Constitution only provided remedy for serious nature of domestic violence. Verbal and emotional abuse, sexual abuse and economic abuse were not covered under the said provisions, which were widely prevalent in the Indian society. Only married women were covered under these legislations. Women facing domestic violence in the parental home were not covered under these provisions. Under the said provisions only punishment can be given to the accused persons. There were not any provisions for sufficient civil reliefs, which could be granted to the victims. The Code of Criminal Procedure, 1973 had provisions for maintenance under Section 125, but maintenance is not the only thing which is required by the victim of domestic violence. A victim of domestic violence need protection, residence, monetary reliefs, compensation etc.

A comprehensive legislation was required, which could focus on the aggrieved women in totality and grant protection to them and also provide civil reliefs like residence, compensation, maintenance etc. There were also women's movements for enactment of domestic violence legislation in India. Contribution of Lawyer's Collective, an NGO, has been remarkable in passing of this Act. Lawyer's Collective has worked as pressure group as well contributed in drafting of the bill. Protection of Women from Domestic Violence Act was finally enacted by the Parliament in 2005.

The High Court of Delhi in **Ram Lakhan Singh Vs. Union of India & Anr; 013SCCOnline Del 4844** has observed on objective behind separate enactment of Protection of Women from Domestic Violence Act, 2005 as under:

"9. The concept of equality between male and female was almost unknown to us before the enactment of the Indian constitution. The status of women in India has undergone several changes over the few decades. Post independence constitution incorporated several articles to ensure gender equality. Article 14 of the Constitution guarantees

equality before law and equal protection of law to any person within the territory of India. <u>Article 15(1)</u> of the Constitution mandates that the State shall not discriminate against any citizen on grounds of religion, race, caste, sex, place of birth or any of them. However, <u>Article 15(3)</u> makes an exception to the rule against discrimination as provided under <u>Article 15(1)</u> and confers a discretionary power on the State to make special provisions for women and children because it recognizes that women in India have been socially and economically handicapped for centuries and therefore so as to bring effective equality between men and women, taking into consideration how the women are subjected to harassment in several forms, the Parliament has enacted several laws, like the <u>Dowry Prohibition Act</u> 1961, <u>The Commission of Sati Prevention Act</u> 1987, <u>Section 498-A</u> was incorporated in <u>the Indian Penal Code</u>, Pre-natal Diagnostic Techniques (Regulation and Prevention of Misuse) Act 1994 was passed which came into force on 01.01.1996.

10. However, in spite of enactment of several laws, the equality guaranteed by the Constitution appears to be only a myth to millions of women for whom life is stalked with various kinds of violence. It was observed that the least visible form of abuse is domestic violence which remains the most widespread and results in the death of several women every year. Though the criminal remedy is available for domestic violence perpetuated on women, under different <u>Sections of Indian Penal Code</u>, the civil law does not address the issue. The Parliament felt it appropriate to have a separate enactment to address the issues arising out of domestic violence and enacted the Protection of Women from <u>Domestic Violence Act</u>, 2005."

High Court of Judicature at Hyderabad in **Jallarapu Laxman Rao and Ors. vs. Jallarapu Pedda Venkateswarlu and Ors.; 2018 (2) ALT (Crl.) 70 (A.P.)** has observed on intention behind enactment of Protection of Women from Domestic Violence Act, 2005 as under:

"*7. When the question of interpretation of a specific provision in the Act came up before this Court, it is the duty of the Court to decide the maintainability of an appeal or revision with reference to the provisions contained in the said enactment based on the object of the*

Act i.e., the Protection of Women from Domestic Violence Act, 2005. The Act is a remedial legislation intended to provide appropriate remedy to the aggrieved person who is subjected to domestic violence as defined in the Act. The present legislations in the country are not sufficient to provide appropriate remedy to the women who are subjected to domestic violence. Domestic violence is sadly a reality in Indian society, a truism, in the Indian patriarchal setup. It became an acceptable practice to abuse women. There may be many reasons for the occurrence of domestic violence. From a feminist standpoint, it could be said that the occurrence of domestic violence against women arises out of the patriarchal setup, the stereotyping of gender roles and the distribution of power, real or perceived, in society. Following such ideology, men are believed to be stronger than women and more powerful. They control women and their lives and as a result of this power play, they may hurt women with impunity. The role of the woman is to accept her 'fate' and the violence employed against her meekly. The Act is a laudable piece of legislation that was enacted in 2005 to tackle this problem. The Act in theory goes a long way towards protection of women in the domestic setup. It is the first substantial step in the direction of vanquishing the questionable public/private distinction traditionally maintained in the law, which has been challenged by feminists time and again. Admittedly, women could earlier approach the Courts under the Indian Penal Code (IPC) in cases of domestic violence. However, the kinds of domestic violence contemplated by this Act and the victims recognized by it, make it more expansive in scope than the IPC. The IPC never used the term domestic violence to refer to this objectionable practice. In fact, the only similar class of offences addressed by the IPC dealt with cruelty to married women. All other instances of domestic violence within the household had to be dealt with under the offences that the respective acts of violence constituted under the IPC without any regard to the gender of the victim. This posed a problem especially where the victims were children or women who were dependent on the assailant. In fact, even where the victim was the wife of the assailant and could approach the Courts under Section 498-A IPC, she would presumably have to move out of her matrimonial home to ensure her safety or face further violence as retaliation. There was no measure in place to allow her to continue staying in her matrimonial home and yet raise her voice against the violence perpetrated against her. This, together with many other problems faced by women in the household, prompted this enactment."

High Court of Gujarat in *Bhartiben Bipinbhai Tamboli Vs. State of Gujarat; 2018(1)Crimes11(Guj.)* has observed on objective of enactment of Protection of Women from Domestic Violence Act, 2005 as under :

"22. Till the year 2005, the remedies available to a victim of domestic violence was limited. The women either had to go to the civil court for a decree of divorce or initiate prosecution in the criminal court for the offence punishable under section 498A of the Indian Penal Code. In both the proceedings, no emergency relief is available to the victim. Also, the relationship outside the marriage was not recogonised. This set of circumstances ensured that a majority of women preferred to suffer in silence, not out of choice but of compulsion. Having regard to all these facts, the Parliament thought fit to enact the Protection of Women from Domestic Violence Act, 2005. The main object of the Act is protection of women from violence inflicted by a man and/or a woman. It is a progressive Act, who's sole intention is to protect the women irrespective of the relationship she shares with the accused. The definition of an aggrieved person under the Act is so wide that it takes within its purview even women who are living with their Partners in a live-in relationship."

CHAPTER I

PRELIMINARY

This chapter covers objective and reasons behind the enactment of this Act, scope of the Act and definitions of various terms used under the Act.

OBJECT OF THE ACT

Statement of objects and reasons -An act to provide for more effective protection of the rights of women guaranteed under the Constitution who are victims of violence of any kind occurring within the family and for matters connected therewith or incidental thereto.

Be it enacted by Parliament in the Fifty Sixth Year of the Republic of India as follows:-

(1) Domestic Violence is undoubtedly a human rights issue and serious deterrent to development. The Vienna Accord of 1994 and the Beijing Declaration and the Platform for Action (1995) have acknowledged this. The United Nations Committee on Convention on Elimination of All Forms of Discrimination against Women (CEDAW) it its General Recommendation No. XII (1989) has recommended that State parties should act to protect women against violence of any kind especially that occurring within family.

(2) The phenomenon of domestic violence is widely prevalent but has remained largely invisible in the public domain. Presently, where a woman is subjected to cruelty by her husband or his relatives, it is an offence under 498-A of the Indian Penal Code. The Civil Law does not however address this phenomenon in its entirety.

(3) It is, therefore, proposed to enact a law keeping in view the rights guaranteed under articles 14, 15 and 21 of the Constitution to provide for a remedy under the civil law which is intended to protect the woman from being victims of domestic violence and to prevent the occurrence of domestic violence in the society.

(4) The Bill, inter alia, seeks to provide for the following:-

(i) It covers those women who are or have been in a relationship with the abuser where both parties have lived together in a shared household and are related by consanguinity, marriage or through a relationship in the nature of marriage or adoption. In addition, relationship with family members living together as a joint family is also included. Even those women who are sisters, widows, mothers, single women, or living with the abuser are entitled to legal protection under the proposed legislation. However, whereas the Bill enables the wife or the female living in a relationship in the nature of marriage to file a complaint under the proposed enactment against any relative of the husband or the male partner, it does not enable any female relative of the husband or the male partner to file a complaint against the wife or the female partner.

(ii) It defines the expression "domestic Violence" to include actual abuse or threat or abuse that is physical, sexual, verbal emotional or economic. Harassment by way of unlawful dowry demands to the woman or her relatives would also be covered under this definition.

(iii) *It provides for rights of women to secure housing. It also provides for the right of woman to reside in her matrimonial home or shared household, whether or not she has any title or rights in such home or household. This right is secured by a residence order, which is passed by the Magistrate.*

(iv) It empowers the Magistrate to pass protection orders in favor of the aggrieved person to prevent the respondent from aiding or committing an act of domestic violence or any other specified act, entering a workplace or any other place frequented by the aggrieved person, attempting to communicate with her , isolating any assets used by both the parties and causing violence to the aggrieved person, her relatives or others who provide her assistance from the domestic violence.

(v) It provides for appointment of Protection Officers and registration of non-governmental organizations as service providers for providing assistance to the aggrieved person with respect to her medical examination, obtaining legal aid, safe shelter etc.

(5) The bill seeks to achieve the above objects. The notes on clauses explain the various provisions contained in the Bill.

Objective of this Act is to give effective protection to women guaranteed under the Constitution, who are victims of violence of any kind occurring within the family. The Constitution grants equal rights to men and women.

The Constitutional guarantee will remain only utopian in nature, if that guarantee is not given effect by the state. Various initiatives had already been taken by the state for protection of women in form of Dowry Prohibition Act, 1961, Sections 498A and 304B of Indian Penal Code, 1860. These initiatives are mainly concerned with protecting women in their matrimonial home. Focus of these legislations was punishment to the accused persons and not on rehabilitation of the victim. There was need of a legislation, which could provide comprehensive reliefs to women against violence occurring within the family, whether in the parental home or in matrimonial home.

UNITED NATIONS INITIATIVES

Discrimination against women is an international phenomena. The United Nations have taken various initiatives for empowerment of women. The some of important initiatives taken by the United Nations are as under:

- Convention of Elimination of all forms of discrimination against women (1989)
- The Vienna Accord (1994)
- Beijing Declaration and the Platform for Action (1995)

THE CONVENTION ON ELIMINATION OF ALL FORMS OF DISCRIMINATION AGAINST WOMEN(CEDAW)

The convention on elimination of all forms of discrimination against women has been adopted by the United Nations General Assembly in 1979. 189 countries have ratified the said convention. It is regarded as international bill of rights for women. This convention is great stride towards gender equality and women empowerment. Article 1 of the convention defines discrimination against women as under:

Article 1

For the purposes of the present Convention "the discrimination against women" shall mean any distinction, exclusion or restriction made on the basis of sex which has the effect or purpose of impairing or nullifying the recognition, enjoyment or exercise by women, irrespective of their marital status, on a basis of equality of men and women, of human rights and fundamental freedoms in the political, economic, social, cultural, civil or any other field.

The convention has 30 sections and divided into six parts. Part I of the Convention deals with non-discrimination, sex stereotypes, and sex trafficking. Part II deals with women's rights in the public sphere with an emphasis on political life, representation and rights to nationality. Part III of the convention deals with the economic and social rights of women particularly on education, employment and health. Part IV of the convention deals with women's right to equality in marriage and family life along with the right of equality before law. Part V of the Convention deals with establishment of the committee on the elimination of discrimination against women as well as the states parties' reporting procedure. Part VI deals with the effects of convention on other treaties, the commitment of the state parties and the administration of the convention.

The convention as such has not dealt specifically with domestic violence, but has focused on elimination of discrimination of all kinds whether political, social and economic. It is a fact that women in many societies and culture do not have equal rights in comparison to that of men. One of the major reasons of violence, including domestic violence, is discrimination prevalent in society against women. If women are politically, socially and economically empowered then automatically it will result in decrease and elimination of incidences of domestic violence.

VIENNA DECLARATION AND PROGRAMME OF ACTION

The World Conference on Human Rights adopted Vienna Declaration and Programme of Action in 1993. It again confirmed the universal nature of human rights. It further declared that all human rights are universal, indivisible, interdependent and inter-related. The Vienna Declaration and Programme of Action *interalia* emphasized on the equal status and human rights of women. The convention also emphasized elimination of violence against women in public and private life. Para 38 of Vienna Declaration and Programme of Action sheds light on the issue of violence against women. Para 38 is reproduced as under:

> "*38.In particular, the World Conference on Human Rights stresses the importance of working towards the elimination of violence against women in public and private life, the elimination of all forms*

of sexual harassment, exploitation and trafficking in women, the elimination of gender bias in the administration of justice and the eradication of any conflicts which may arise between the rights of women and the harmful effects of certain traditional or customary practices, cultural prejudices and religious extremism. The World Conference on Human Rights calls upon the General Assembly to adopt the draft declaration on violence against women and urges States to combat violence against women in accordance with its provisions. Violations of the human rights of women in situations of armed conflict are violations of the fundamental principles of international human rights and humanitarian law. All violations of this kind, including in particular murder, systematic rape, sexual slavery, and forced pregnancy, require a particularly effective response."

Thus Vienna Declaration was an important instrument against violence against women. Through this Declaration, the states were urged to combat violence against women.

BEIJING DECLARATION AND PLATFORM FOR ACTION

Fourth World Conference on Women was held at Beijing, China in 1995. Beijing Declaration and Platform of Action was adopted at the said conference, which is one of the most progressive blueprint for advancing women's rights. The Beijing Declaration and platform for action is a comprehensive document for realizing gender equality and empowerment of women. Beijing Declaration and Platform for Action advocates intervention by various stakeholders like Governments, Non-governmental Organisations, International Organisations etc. in 12 critical areas i.e. poverty, education and training, health, violence, armed conflict, economy, power and decision making, institutional mechanism for advancement of women, human rights, media, environment and the girl child.

The issue of violence against women, including domestic violence, has been emphasized under the Beijing Declaration and Platform for Action. The Beijing Declaration showed its determination to prevent and eliminate all forms of violence against women and girls.

The platform of Action suggested strategic actions by various stakeholders including Governments, Non-governmental organizations and

International Organizations. One of important feature of the Platform of Action was that the Governments were directed inter alia to take legislative measures to eliminate violence against women.

Aforesaid international initiatives were also relevant factors for the enactment of Protection of Women from Domestic Violence Act, 2005. Indian Courts have taken note of these international initiatives while interpreting the provisions of the Protection of Women from Domestic Violence Act, 2005. High Court of Delhi in *Aruna Parmod Shah Vs. Union of India; 2008(102)DRJ543* has observed as under:

> *"4. Domestic violence is a worldwide phenomenon and has been discussed in International fora, including the Vienna Accord of 1994 and the Beijing Declaration and the Platform for Action (1995). The United Nations Committee Convention on Elimination of All Forms of Discrimination against Women (CEDAW) has recommended that States should act to protect women against violence of any kind, especially that occurring within the family. There is a perception, not unfounded or unjustified, that the lot and fate of women in India is an abjectly dismal one, which requires bringing into place, on an urgent basis, protective and ameliorative measures against exploitation of women. The argument that the Act is ultra virus the Constitution of India because it accords protection only to women and not to men, is therefore, wholly devoid of any merit. We do not rule out the possibility of a man becoming the victim of domestic violence, but such cases would be few and far between, thus not requiring or justifying the protection of parliament."*

Cielo

INADEQUACY OF DOMESTIC LEGAL FRAMEWORK TO DEAL WITH DOMESTIC VIOLENCE

Domestic violence has been widely prevalent in Indian society, but it has been largely invisible in the public domain. Although various laws have been enacted for protection of women, as yet they were not sufficient to deal with violence occurring within the family. Dowry Prohibition Act, 1861, Section 498A & 304B of the Indian Penal Code, 1860, and Section 125 of Code of Criminal Procedure, 1973 are major interventions for protection of women. These interventions have definitely helped in providing reliefs to women, but they have been unsuccessful in providing a comprehensive solution to deal with domestic violence suffered by women.

DOWRY PROHIBITION ACT, 1961

Dowry has grown as deep rooted social evil because of social and cultural factors. Dowry demand by in-laws of women is widely prevalent in India. Women in India frequently face domestic violence in connection with demand of dowry. Women are taunted, harassed, beaten and even killed for not bringing sufficient dowry. Women are coerced to demand dowry from their parents. The Supreme Court in **Kamlesh Panjiyar Vs. State of Bihar; (2005)2SCC388** has observed as under:

> "2. *Marriages are made in heaven, is an adage. A bride leaves the parental home for the matrimonial home, leaving behind sweet memories therewith a hope that she will see a new world full of love in her groom's house. She leaves behind not only her memories, but also her surname, gotra and maidenhood. She expects not only to be a daughter-in-law, but a daughter in fact. Alas! the alarming rise in the number of cases involving harassment to the newly wed girls for dowry shatters the dreams. In-laws are characterized to be outlaws for perpetrating terrorism which destroys the matrimonial home. The terrorist is dowry, and it is spreading tentacles in every possible direction."*

To fight with this social evil of dowry, Dowry Prohibition Act, 1961 was enacted to prohibit giving or taking of dowry. Dowry was defined as property or valuable security given by one party, parents of one party or any other person to other party, parents of other party or any other person before the marriage, at the time of marriage or after the marriage in connection of marriage of parties. Giving, taking and abetment of dowry were made punishable with minimum imprisonment of 5 years and with fine not less than fifteen thousand or amount of value of such dowry, whichever was more. Demand of dowry suas also made punishable with imprisonment of minimum 6 months which may extend to two years and fine which may extend to ten thousand rupees.

Dowry Prohibition Act, 1961 was a progressive legislation but it has not been an effective legislation as collection of evidence regarding to giving and taking of dowry is difficult. Presents given to the bride or bridegroom have been exempted subject to the condition that a list of presents shall be prepared. As per the Act, such presents have to be customary in nature and value of presents should not be excessive with regard to financial status of such person. It is uphill task for any person to judge what is a financial capacity of a person is and whether presents given by him are in excess of his capacity.

SECTION 498A OF INDIAN PENAL CODE, 1860

In light of increasing dowry deaths, Parliament vide the Criminal Law (Second) Amendment Act, 1983, inserted 498A in Indian Penal Code, 1860. The said amendment protects married women against cruelties inflicted by husband and his relatives. Cruelties inflicted by the husband and his relatives were made punishable up to three years imprisonment. Section 498A of the Indian Penal Code, 1860 reads as under:

498A. Husband or relative of husband of a woman subjecting her to cruelty – Whoever, being the husband or the relative of the husband of a woman, subjects such woman to cruelty shall be punishable with imprisonment for a term which may extend to three years and shall also be liable to fine.

Explanation.-For the purpose of this section, "cruelty" means- (a) any willful conduct which is of such a nature as is likely to drive the woman to commit suicide or to cause grave injury or danger to life, limb or health (whether mental or physical) of woman; or (b) harassment of the woman where such harassment is with a view to coercing her or any person related to her to meet any unlawful demand for any property or valuable security or is on account of failure by her or any person related to her to meet such demand.

Under section 498A of the Indian Penal Code, 1860, husband and relatives of husband, who subject a woman to cruelty, can be prosecuted. Cruelty has been defined as willful conduct of the husband or relative of the husband which drives woman to commit suicide or to cause grave injury or danger to life, limb or health (whether mental or physical) of woman. Cruelty also includes harassment in form of coercion by husband or relative of the husband for unlawful demand of property or valuable security or harassment by husband or relative of the husband for non-fulfillment of such unlawful demand of property or valuable security

Although introduction of 498A of Indian Penal Code, 1860 was a progressive step in fighting domestic violence against women, it has certain limitations. *Firstly*, definition of cruelty did not cover various aspects of domestic violence. *Secondly*, only married women have been covered Section 498A and hence only domestic violence perpetrated within matrimonial home was addressed under this provision. *Thirdly*, it is only a penal remedy and does not provide any constructive support to the aggrieved women. Punishment meted out to an accused does not in any way help in rehabilitation of victims of domestic violence. An aggrieved woman is in need of various kinds of reliefs in forms of protection, maintenance, residence, Compensation etc.

SECTION 304 B OF INDIAN PENAL CODE

Dowry deaths are worst kind of crime. Despite enactment of Dowry Prohibition Act, 1961 and inclusion of 498 A in the Indian Penal Code, 1860, instances of dowry deaths were increasing in the society. In case of dowry deaths, generally family members are involved and direct evidence for such crime is not always available. In such a scenario need was felt for creating a new offence of dowry death. Section 304 B was introduced in the Indian Penal Code, 1860 vide Dowry Prohibition (Amendment) Act, 1986. Section 304 B of Indian Penal Code, 1860 reads as under:

304B. Dowry death: (1) Where death of a woman is caused by any burns or bodily injury or occurs otherwise than under normal circumstances within seven years of her marriage and it is shown than soon before her death she was subjected to cruelty or harassment by her husband or nay relative of her husband or any relative of her husband for, or in connection with, any demand for dowry, such death shall be called "dowry death" and such husband or relative shall be deemed to have caused her deaths.

Explanation: For Purpose of this sub-section, "dowry" shall have the same meaning as in section 2 of the Dowry Prohibition Act, 1961 (28 of 1961).

(2) Whoever commits dowry death shall be punished with imprisonment for a term which shall not be less than seven years but which may extend to imprisonment for life.

Under section 304 B of Indian Penal Code, 1860, dowry has been given the same meaning as given in Dowry Prohibition Act, 1961. For a crime to be covered in under Section 304 B four ingredients are necessary. *Firstly,* death of a woman is either by burns or by bodily injury or otherwise than under normal circumstances, *Secondly*, It should be within seven years of marriage, *Thirdly* it should be shown that soon before her death she was subjected to cruelty or harassment by husband or any relative of husband, *Fourthly* such harassment or cruelty should pertain to demand for dowry. Minimum punishment under the said provision is 7 years which may extend to imprisonment for life.

Indian Evidence Act, 1872 was also amended to incorporate Section 113 B. Section 113B of the Indian Evidence Act reads as under:

113B. Presumption as to dowry death: When the question is whether a person has committed the dowry death of a woman and it is shown that soon before her death such woman has been subjected by such person to cruelty or harassment for , or in connection with, any demand for dowry, the Court shall presume that such person had caused the dowry death.

Explanation: For the purposes of this section "dowry death" shall have the same meaning as in section 304B of Indian Penal Code (45 of 1860).

Under section 113B of Indian Evidence Act, 1872, a presumption was created that if woman has been subjected to cruelty or harassment for, or in connection with demand for dowry by any person; such person has caused dowry death. This section was introduced in light of the fact that dowry death is caused by close family members and availability of evidence is difficult in such circumstances.

Section 304B of Indian Penal Code, 1860 addresses issues of serious nature of domestic violence in form of dowry death. But the focus of this Section is also on punishment of accused and not on protection and rehabilitation of the victim.

SECTION 125 OF CODE OF CRIMINAL PROCEDURE, 1973

Section 125 of Code of Criminal Procedure provides civil reliefs in form maintenance to wives, children and parents. It is one of the earliest remedies available under law which provides safety to women against economic deprivation. Being a criminal legislation, it is applicable to everyone irrespective of their personal laws. A woman can also avail interim maintenance under Section 125 of Code of Criminal Procedure, 1973 during pendency of proceedings.

Section 125 of Code of Criminal Procedure, 1973 has been one of most availed sections by women for availing security against economic deprivation in form of maintenance. But it only provides partial relief to women against economic deprivation. It does not provide women right to enjoy economic resources of the shared household, right to residence, compensation, other monetary reliefs etc.

ARTICLE 14, 15 & 21 OF.THE CONSTITUTION

The Constitution grants equal rights to both men and women. Constitution empowers the state to make special provisions for women as women have faced discrimination in the past and some initiatives are required for betterment of their position in the society.

Article 14 stipulates that state shall not deny to any person equality before law or the equal protection of laws within the territory of India. Article 15 stipulates that the state shall not discriminate against any citizen on grounds only of religion, race, caste, sex, place of birth or any of them.

In *Shayara Bano vs. Union of India and Ors (2017) 9 SCC 1* the Supreme Court has observed that the Indian State is committed to gender equality. Relevant para of the said judgment reads as under :

> *"186. We have considered the submissions advanced on behalf of the petitioners, pointedly with reference to international conventions and declarations. We have not the least doubt, that the Indian State is committed to gender equality. This is clear mandate of Article 14 of the Constitution. India is also committed to eradicate discrimination on the ground of sex. Article 15 and 16 of the Constitution, prohibit any kind of discrimination on the basis of sex. There is therefore no reason or necessity while examining the issue of 'talaq-e-biddat' to fall back upon international conventions and declarations."*

Article 15 (3) stipulates that nothing in this article shall prevent the state from making any special provision for women and children. Supreme Court in *Govt. of A.P. vs. P.B. Vijaykumar (1995)4SCC520*has observed that Article 15(3) has been placed under Article 15 to bring effective equality between men and women. Relevant para reads as under:

> *"7. The insertion of Clause (3) of Article 15 in relation to women is recognition of the fact that for centuries, women of this country have been socially and economically handicapped. As a result, they are*

unable to participate in the socio-economic activities of the nation on a footing of equality. It is in order to eliminate this socio-economic backwardness of women and to empower them in a manner that would bring about effective equality between men and women that Article15(3) is placed in Article 15. Its object is to strengthen and improve the status of women. An important limb of this concept of gender equality is creating job opportunities for women. To say that under Article 15(3), job opportunities for women cannot be created would be to cut at the very root of the underlying inspiration behind this Article. Making special provisions for women in respect of employment or posts under the State is an integral part of Article 15(3). This power conferred under Article 15(3) is not whittled down in any manner by Article 16. "

Article 21 stipulates that no person shall be deprived of his life or personal liberty except according to procedure established by law. Article 21 has been liberally interpreted by courts and it has been held that Right to enjoy life through limbs and faculties and right to dignified life is covered under Article 21 of the Constitution of India.

In ***Francis Coralie Mullin vs. Administrator, Union Territory of Delhi; 1981 AIR 746*** the Supreme Court has held that right to life includes right to enjoy life through limb and faculties:

"*7. Now obviously, the right to life enshrined in Article 21 cannot be restricted to mere animal existence. It means something much more than just physical survival.*

In Kharak Singh v. State of Uttar Pradesh [1964] 1 S.C.R. 232 Subba Rao J. quoted with approval the following passage from the judgment of Field J. in Munn v. Illinois [1877] 94 U.S. 113 to emphasize the quality of life covered by Article 21.

By the term "life" as here used something more is meant than mere animal existence. The inhibition against its deprivation extends to all those limbs and faculties by which life is enjoyed. The provision equally prohibits the mutilation of the body or amputation of an arm or leg or the putting out of an eye or the destruction of any other organ of the body through which the soul communicates with the outer world.

and this passage was again accepted as laying down the correct law by the Constitution Bench of this Court in the first Sunil Batra case (supra). Every limb or faculty through which life is enjoyed is thus protected by Article 21 and a fortiori, this would include the faculties of thinking and feeling. Now deprivation which is inhibited by Article 21 may be total or partial, neither any limb or faculty can be totally destroyed nor can it be partially damaged. Moreover it is every kind of deprivation that is hit by Article 21, whether such deprivation be permanent or temporary and, furthermore, deprivation is not an act which is complete once and for all: it is a continuing act and so long as it lasts, it must be in accordance with procedure established by law. It is therefore clear that any act which damages or injures or interferes with the use of, any limb or faculty of a person, either permanently or even temporarily, would be within the inhibition of Article 21."

Women have fundamental right to decide her sexual autonomy. Marriage does not mean ceding sexual automony to husband. In **Joseph Shine vs. Union of India; AIR2018SC4898** the Supreme Court has observed as under:

"59. In criminalizing adultery, the legislature has imposed its imprimatur on the control by a man over the sexuality of his spouse. In doing that, the statutory provision fails to meet the touch stone of Article 21. Section 497 deprives a woman of her autonomy, dignity and privacy. It compounds the encroachment on her right to life and personal liberty by adopting a notion of marriage which subverts true equality. Equality is subverted by lending the sanctions of the penal law to a gender biased approach to the relationship of a man and a woman. The statute confounds paternalism as an instrument for protecting marital stability. It defines the sanctity of marriage in terms of hierarchical ordering which is skewed against the woman. The law gives unequal voices to partners in a relationship.

This judgment has dwelt on the importance of sexual autonomy as a value which is integral to life and personal liberty under Article 21. Individuals in a relationship, whether within or outside marriage, have a legitimate expectation that each will provide to other the same element of companionship and respect for choices for sexual autonomy, it must be emphasized is founded on the equality between spouses and partners and the recognition by each of them of the dignity of the other. Control over sexuality attaches to the human element in each individual. Marriage- whether it be a sacrament or contract- does not result in ceding of the autonomy of one spouse to another."

In ***Santistar Builder v. N.KI. Totame; (1990) 1 SCC 520*** the Supreme Court has held that Right to Shelter is also a fundamental right. The relevant para is reproduced as under:

"9. Basic needs of man have traditionally been accepted to be three- food, clothing and shelter. The right to life is guaranteed in any civilized society. That would take within its sweep the right to food, the right to clothing, the right to decent environment and a reasonable accommodation to live in. The difference between the need of an animal and a human being for shelter has to be kept in view. For the animal it is the bare protection of the body; for a human being it has to be a suitable accommodation which would allow him to grow in every aspect - physical, mental and intellectual. The Constitution aims at ensuring fuller development of every child. That would be possible only if the child is in a proper home. It is not necessary that every citizen must be ensured of living in a well- built comfortable house but a reasonable home particularly for people in India can even be mud-built thatched house or a mud- built fire-proof accommodation."

Article 21 has been also interpreted to include right to dignity. A woman has right to lead a dignified life. In ***State of Madhya Pradesh vs. Madanlal; (2015) 7 SCC 681***, the Supreme Court observed as under:

"16. The aforesaid view was expressed while dealing with the imposition of sentence. We would like to clearly state that in a case of rape or attempt of rape, the conception of compromise under no circumstances can really be thought of. These are crimes against the body of a woman which is her own temple. These are offences which suffocate the breath of life and sully the reputation. And reputation, needless to emphasize, is the richest jewel one can conceive of in life. No one would allow it to be extinguished. When a human frame is

defiled, the "purest treasure", is lost. Dignity of a woman is a part of her non-perishable and immortal self and no one should ever think of painting it in clay. There cannot be a compromise or settlement as it would be against her honour which matters the most. It is sacrosanct. Sometimes solace is given that the perpetrator of the crime has acceded to enter into wedlock with her which is nothing but putting pressure in an adroit manner; and we say with emphasis that the Courts are to remain absolutely away from this subterfuge to adopt a soft approach to the case, for any kind of liberal approach has to be put in the compartment of spectacular error. Or to put it differently, it would be in the realm of a sanctuary of error. We are compelled to say so as such an attitude reflects lack of sensibility towards the dignity, the elan vital, of a woman. Any kind of liberal approach or thought of mediation in this regard is thoroughly and completely sans legal permissibility. "

The Supreme Court in *Justice K.S.Puttaswamy (Retd) vs Union of India and Ors.; (2017) 10 SCC 1* has held that individual is focal point of the Constitution. Human dignity is an integral part of the Constitution. The Supreme Court has observed as under:

" 96. over the last four decades, our constitutional jurisprudence has recognized the inseparable relationship between protection of life and liberty with dignity. Dignity as a constitutional value finds expression in the Preamble. The constitutional vision seeks the realization of justice (social, economic and political); liberty (of thought, expression, belief, faith and worship); equality (as a guarantee against arbitrary treatment of individuals) and fraternity (which assures a life of dignity to every individual). These constitutional precepts exist in unity to facilitate a humane and compassionate society. The individual is the focal point of the Constitution because it is in the realization of individual rights that the collective well being of the community is determined. Human dignity is an integral part of the Constitution. Reflections of dignity are found in the guarantee against arbitrariness (Article 14), the lamps of freedom (Article 19) and in the right to life and personal liberty (Article 21). "

Central and State Governments have taken various legislative and policy initiatives to implement the Constitutional mandate for empowerment and emancipation of women. The Protection of Women from Domestic Violence Act, 2005 is another one of the landmark initiative to give effect to Constitutional mandate under Article 14, 15 and Article 21.

SHORT TITLE EXTENT AND COMMENCEMENT

1. Short title, extent and commencement- (1) This act may be called the Protection of Women from Domestic Violence Act, 2005.

(2) It extends to the whole of India.

(3) It shall come into force on such date as the Central Government may, by notification in the Official Gazette, appoint.

This Act has been titled as "The Protection of Women from Domestic Violence Act, 2005". The title of this Act itself suggests that this Act has been enacted for protection of women from domestic violence. The Act extends to whole of India. This Act was brought into force from 26.10.2006 vide Central Government notification dated 17.10.2006.

DEFINITIONS

2.Definitions: In this Act, unless the context otherwise requires:-

(a) "aggrieved person" means any woman who is, or has been in a domestic relationship with the respondent and who alleges to have been subjected to any act of domestic violence by the respondent.

"Aggrieved person" can be only a woman. A man cannot claim to be aggrieved person under this Act. Such woman should be currently living or should have lived in domestic relationship with the Respondent. The term "domestic relationship" has been defined under Section 2(f) of the Act. The term "respondent" has been defined under Section 2(q) of the Act. Only such women are covered under the definition of "aggrieved person" who have been subjected to domestic violence by the respondent. The term "domestic violence" has been defined under Section 3 of the Act.

Restrictive interpretation cannot be given to term "woman" in the definition of "aggrieved person". Aggrieved person includes all women who are in domestic relationship with respondent. As per definition of "domestic relationship" under section 2 (f), domestic relationship are relationship between two persons when they are related by consanguinity, marriage or through a relationship in the nature of marriage, adoption or are family members living together as a joint family. Thus not only marital relationship, but a wide range of relationships have been covered under the definition of "domestic relationship".

The High Court of Kerala in **Bismi Sainudheen vs. P.K. Nabeesa Beevi & Ors; 2014 CriLJ 904**has held that definition of "aggrieved person" cannot be interpreted by giving a narrow meaning as "wife" only :

> *"Thus , on a consideration of the circumstances under which the Act promulgated and the objects sought to be achieved, it is crystal clear that the main object is to protect the women as a whole and according to me, that is why the Act itself named and projected as "The protection of Women from Domestic Violence Act". It is relevant to note that, Section 2 (a) of the Act defines an "aggrieved person" which reads as follows.*
>
> *"aggrieved person" means any woman who is, or has been, in a domestic relationship with the Respondent and who alleges to have been subjected any act of domestic violence by the respondent."*
>
> *A plain reading of the section indicates, particularly in view of the emphasized portion of the object, that any woman in a domestic relationship with the respondent can invoke the provisions of the Act, provided, the other conditions are satisfied. It is relevant to note that the definitions "aggrieved person" is not confined to a lady, or woman, based upon her marital status alone. So, the definition of "aggrieved person" cannot be interpreted by giving a narrow meaning as "wife" only."*

An Application of only "aggrieved person" under Section 12 of this Act is maintainable before Court. If a person is not covered under the definition of the "aggrieved person", Application will not be maintainable. Bombay High Court in **Mr. Prakash Kumar Singhee vs. Ms. Amrapali Singhee; 2018(2) Crimes333(Bom.)** has observed as under:

> *"14. Learned counsel Mrs.Sarnaik is perfectly justified in submitting that the provisions under the said enactment cannot be invoked unless the party alleges an act of domestic violence and approach the Court in the capacity as an "aggrieved person". Though the application filed by the applicant can be entertained in the pending*

proceedings under the <u>Specific Relief Act</u>, while entertaining an application which is filed Sub-section-1 of Section- 12, it is imperative that the person approaching the Court is an "aggrieved person". Though the Family Court in the impugned order has noted the submissions advanced on behalf of the petitioner-husband that the preliminary requirement of the domestic violence has not been proved by the petitioner and therefore application is not maintainable, the Family Court did not pay any heed to the said submission and rather proceeded to decide the matter on its own merits. The Court has merely noted that as per provision of Section-20 of the D.V. Act aggrieved by had claimed monetary relief for herself and her children however, a whether the applicant is an "aggrieved person" has not at all been considered by the Family Court. Though the Act of Domestic Violence would be established after rendering evidence before the Court, at least the Court prima facie must be satisfied that the person approaching is as an "aggrieved person". It is not every person who can invoke the jurisdiction of the Court under the 2005 Act, simply for claiming maintenance, as the purpose of the enactment is to protect rights of women who are victims of violence of any kind occurring within the family. The Court has refused to consider the said aspect of the matter."

A woman remains aggrieved person even after decree of judicial separation. Judicial separation does not terminate domestic relationship. Supreme Court in**Krishna Bhatacharjee vs Sarathi Choudhury And Anr; (2016) 2 SCC 705**has observed as under:

"18. The core issue that is requisite to be addressed is whether the appellant has ceased to be an "aggrieved person" because of the decree of judicial separation. Once the decree of divorce is passed, the status of the parties becomes different, but that is not so when there is a decree for judicial separation. A three-Judge Bench in Jeet Singh and Others vs. State of U.P. and Others though in a different context, adverted to the concept of judicial separation and ruled that the judicial separation creates rights and obligations. A decree or an order for judicial separation permits the parties to live apart. There would be no obligation for either party to cohabit with the

other. Mutual rights and obligations arising out of a marriage are suspended. The decree however, does not sever or dissolve the marriage. It affords an opportunity for reconciliation and adjustment. Though judicial separation after a certain period may become a ground for divorce, it is not necessary and the parties are not bound to have recourse to that remedy and the parties can live keeping their status as wife and husband till their lifetime."

(b) "child" means any person below the age of eighteen years and includes any adopted, step or foster child;

A child has been defined as any person, who is below eighteen years. Child includes adopted child, step child or foster child.

(c) "compensation order" means an order granted in terms of section 22;

(d) "custody order" means an order granted in terms of section 21;

(e)"domestic incident report" means a report made in the prescribed form on receipt of a complaint of domestic violence from an aggrieved person;

Domestic incident report is a form which captures details of the domestic violence incidences i.e. sexual violence, economic violence, verbal and emotional abuse, dowry related harassment, domestic violence upon children on the aggrieved person. It also captures details of orders and assistance, which an aggrieved person may seek from the magistrate. Domestic incident report assists the magistrate and other relevant authorities in determining interventions required for providing reliefs to the aggrieved person.

Under the Section 9 (1) (b) of the Act, the protection officer has to prepare a domestic incident report. Section 37 (2) (c) of the Act empowers the Central Government to make rules in respect of form and the manner in which a domestic incident report may be made under clause 1(b) of Section 9.

Rule 5 of the Protection of Women from Domestic Violence Rules, 2006 provides procedure for preparation of domestic incident report. Rule 5 is reproduced as under:

(5) Domestic Incident Reports- (1) upon receipt of a Complaint of domestic violence, the Protection Officer shall prepare a domestic incident report in Form I and submit the same to the Magistrate and forward copies thereof to the Police Officer in charge of the Police Station within the local limits of jurisdiction of which the domestic violence alleged to have been

committed has taken place and to the service providers in that area.

(2) Upon a request of any aggrieved person, a service provider may record a domestic incident report in Form I, and forward a copy thereof to the magistrate and protection officer having jurisdiction in the area where the domestic violence is alleged to have taken place.

As per Rule 5, when a protection officer receives a complaint, she has to prepare a domestic incident report in Form I and submit the same to the magistrate. The protection officer has also to send a copy of the same to the jurisdictional police station. A service provider can also prepare domestic incident report and submit it to the magistrate. The service provider may also send a copy of the same to the jurisdictional police station.

Submission of domestic incident report in Form I is only procedural in nature and this cannot be ground of dismissal of application by the magistrate. The Uttarakhand High Court in **Baldev Raj Gagneja and Ors. vs. Smt. Neha Gagneja; Criminal Misc. Application No. 171 of 2009** has observed as under:

> *"17. From the perusal of the provisions made under Section 12(1) read with Rule 5, 1 AM of the view that submission of the report in Form 1 is only procedural in nature. If Protection Officer fails to submit his report strictly as per Rule 5 in Form 1, then it is always open to the Magistrate to call for further report from the Protection Officer in the Form 1. However, in any event, Magistrate should not throw the application in dustbin only on the ground of non-compliance of the Rule 5 of the Act. If report is not submitted in Form 1 as provided under Rule 5, then claimant/aggrieved person would be deprived from justice for the fault of the Protection Officer, which cannot be said to be justified. Moreover, this is settled principle of law that technicalities should not come in the way of dispensing justice.*
>
> *18. Meaning thereby purpose of report of the Protection Officer is to assist the Magistrate. Hence procedure error committed by the Protection Officer in submitting the report should not be made ground to reject the application moved under Section 12 before the Magistrate."*

(f) "domestic relationship" means a relationship between two persons who live or have, at any point of time, lived together in a shared household, when they are related by consanguinity, marriage or through a relationship in the

nature of marriage, adoption or are family members living together as a joint family.

For a relationship to be "domestic relationship" between two persons, there should exist a relationship of consanguinity, marriage or a relationship in nature of marriage, adoption or are family members living to-gather as a joint family. Such persons should live presently in a shared household or at any point of time have lived together in a shared household.

It is evident from the definition of "domestic relationship" that "domestic relationship" includes a wide range of relationships. Domestic relationship includes relationship by consanguinity.

Relationship by consanguinity is a relationship between persons, who have descended from the same ancestor. Relationship by consanguinity can be lineal consanguinity or collateral consanguinity. Lineal consanguinity is a relationship in direct line such as child, parent and grandparents. It may be determined upward or downward. It may be determined upward as in case of son, father and grandfather or it may be determined downward as in case of son, grandson or great grandson. Collateral consanguinity is a remote relationship between persons who are related by common ancestor but do not descend from same ancestor such as cousins.

Domestic relationship includes marital relationship as well as relationship in nature of marriage. Relationship in nature of marriage has been incorporated by the legislature keeping in view current social reality. Relationship in nature of marriage covers certain live-in relationships but not all live-in relationships.

Domestic relationship also includes relationship by adoption.

Domestic relationship also includes relationship between family members living together as joint family members. Joint family has not been defined under the Act. Joint family has been used in generic way and cannot be given restrictive meaning like Hindu undivided family.

Supreme Court in **Hiral P. Harsora and Ors. vs. Kusum Narottamdas Harsora And Ors; (2016)10SCC165** has observed as under:

> "*18. It will be noticed that the definition of "domestic relationship" contained in Section 2(f) is a very wide one. It is a relationship between persons who live or have lived together in a shared household and are related in any one of four ways-blood, marriage or a relationship in the nature of marriage, adoption, or family members of a joint family. A reading of these definitions makes it clear that*

domestic relationships involve persons belonging to both sexes and includes persons related by blood or marriage. This necessarily brings within such domestic relationships male as well as female in-laws, quite apart from male and female members of a family related by blood. Equally, a shared household includes a household which belongs to a joint family of which the Respondent is a member. As has been rightly pointed out by Ms. Arora, even before the 2005 Act was brought into force on 26.10.2006, the Hindu Succession Act, 1956 was amended, by which Section 6 was amended, with effect from 9.9.2005, to make females coparceners of a joint Hindu family and so have a right by birth in the property of such joint family. This being the case, when a member of a joint Hindu family will now include a female coparcener as well, the restricted definition contained in Section 2(q) has necessarily to be given a relook, given that the definition of 'shared household' in Section 2(s) of the Act would include a household which may belong to a joint family of which the Respondent is a member. The aggrieved person can therefore make, after 2006, her sister, for example, a Respondent, if the Hindu Succession Act amendment is to be looked at. But such is not the case Under Section 2(q) of the 2005 Act, as the main part of Section 2(q) continues to read "adult male person", while Section 2(s) would include such female coparcener as a Respondent, being a member of a joint family. This is one glaring anomaly which we have to address in the course of our judgment. "

Cielo

RELATIONSHIP IN NATURE OF MARRIAGE

The term "relationship in nature of marriage" has not been defined under the Act. The termhas been included by the legislature in view of changing social scenario in India. Even though the culture of live-in has not as yet been widely accepted by society in India, there are increasing instances of live-in relationships. Women in live-in relationships are also in need of protection. But all live-in relationships are not covered under the definitions of domestic relationship. As legislature has not defined the term, one will have to rely on the interpretation supplied by Judiciary.

In **Velusamy vs. D. Patchaiammal; (2010) 10 SCC 469** the Supreme Court has prescribed certain conditions which must be fulfilled for a relationship to be covered under "relationship in nature of marriage".

"32. Some countries in the world recognize common law marriages. A common law marriage, sometimes called de facto marriage, or informal marriage is recognized in some countries as a marriage though no legally recognized marriage ceremony is performed or civil marriage contract is entered into or the marriage registered in a civil registry (see details on Google).

33. In our opinion a 'relationship in the nature of marriage' is akin to a common law marriage. Common law marriages require that although not being formally married:

(a) The couple must hold themselves out to society as being akin to spouses.

(b) They must be of legal age to marry.

(c) They must be otherwise qualified to enter into a legal marriage, including being unmarried.

(d) They must have voluntarily cohabited and held themselves out to the world as being akin to spouses for a significant period of time.

(see 'Common Law Marriage' in Wikipedia on Google)

In our opinion a 'relationship in the nature of marriage' under the 2005 Act must also fulfill the above requirements, and in addition the parties must have lived together in a 'shared household' as defined in Section 2(s) of the Act. Merely spending weekends together or a one night stand would not make it a 'domestic relationship'.

34. In our opinion not all live in relationships will amount to a relationship in the nature of marriage to get the benefit of the Act of 2005. To get such benefit the conditions mentioned by us above must be satisfied, and this has to be proved by evidence. If a man has a 'keep' whom he maintains financially and uses mainly for sexual purpose and/or as a servant it would not, in our opinion, be a relationship in the nature of marriage."

The Supreme Court in ***Indra Sharma vs V.K.V. Sarma; (2013) 15 SCC 755*** has also provided certain guidelines to determine whether a relationship is "relationship in nature of marriage".

"55. We may, on the basis of above discussion cull out some guidelines for testing under what circumstances, a live-in relationship

will fall within the expression "relationship in the nature of marriage" Under Section 2(f) of the DV Act. The guidelines, of course, are not exhaustive, but will definitely give some insight to such relationships.

(1) Duration of period of relationship

Section 2(f) of the DV Act has used the expression "at any point of time", which means a reasonable period of time to maintain and continue a relationship which may vary from case to case, depending upon the fact situation.

(2) Shared household

The expression has been defined Under Section 2(s) of the DV Act and, hence, need no further elaboration.

(3) Pooling of Resources and Financial Arrangements

Supporting each other, or any one of them, financially, sharing bank accounts, acquiring immovable properties in joint names or in the name of the woman, long term investments in business, shares in separate and joint names, so as to have a long standing relationship, may be a guiding factor.

(4) Domestic Arrangements

Entrusting the responsibility, especially on the woman to run the home, do the household activities like cleaning, cooking, maintaining or up keeping the house, etc. is an indication of a relationship in the nature of marriage.

(5) Sexual Relationship

Marriage like relationship refers to sexual relationship, not just for pleasure, but for emotional and intimate relationship, for procreation of children, so as to give emotional support, companionship and also material affection, caring etc.

(6) Children

Having children is a strong indication of a relationship in the nature of marriage. Parties, therefore, intend to have a long standing relationship. Sharing the responsibility for bringing up and supporting them is also a strong indication.

(7) Socialization in Public

Holding out to the public and socializing with friends, relations and others, as if they are husband and wife is a strong circumstance to hold the relationship is in the nature of marriage.

(8) Intention and conduct of the parties

Common intention of parties as to what their relationship is to be and to involve, and as to their respective roles and responsibilities, primarily determines the nature of that relationship."

(g) "domestic violence" has the same meaning as assigned to it in section 3;

(h) "dowry" shall have the same meaning as assigned to it in section 2 of the Dowry Prohibition Act, 1961 (28 of 1961)

The Act does not provide definition of the term "dowry", but states that "dowry" shall have same meaning as assigned to it in Section 2 of the Dowry Prohibition Act, 1961. "Dowry" has been defined under Section 2 of the Dowry Prohibition Act, 1961 as under:

2. In this Act, "dowry" means any property or valuable security given or agreed to be given either directly or indirectly.

(a) By one party to a marriage to the other party to the marriage, or

(b) By the parent of either party to a marriage or by any other person, to either party to the marriage or to any other person, at or before or any time after the marriage in connection with the marriage of the said parties, but does not include dower or mahr in the case of persons to whom the Muslim Personal Law (Shariat) applies.

Explanation II. — The expression "valuable security" has the same meaning as in section 30 of the Indian Penal Code (45 of 1860).

The Supreme Court in **Satvir Singh And Ors Vs. State of Punjab (2001)8SCC633** has observed on the scope of definition of dowry as under:

"21. Thus, there are three occasions related to dowry. One is before the marriage, second is at the time of marriage and the third is "at any time" after the marriage. The third occasion may appear to be an unending period. But the crucial words are "in connection with the marriage of the said parties". This means that giving or agreeing to give any property or valuable security on any of the above three stages should have been in connection with the marriage of the parties. There can be many other instances for payment of money or giving property as between the spouses. For example, some customary payments in connection with birth of a child or other ceremonies are prevalent in different societies. Such payments are not enveloped within the ambit of "dowry". Hence the dowry mentioned in Section 304B should be any property or valuable security given or agreed to

be given in connection with the marriage."

(i)"Magistrate" means the Judicial Magistrate of the first class or as the case may be, the Metropolitan Magistrate, exercising jurisdiction under the Code of Criminal Procedure, 1973 (2 of 1974) in the area where the aggrieved person resides temporarily or otherwise or the respondent resides or the domestic violence is alleged to have taken place.

(j)"Medical facility" means such facility as may be notified by the State Government to be a medical facility for the purpose of this Act;

Medical facility has to be notified by the State Government under this Act. Under Section 7 of this Act, if aggrieved person or on her behalf any protection officer or service provider approaches the medical facility to provide medical aid, it is duty of the medical facility to provide medical aid.

(k) "monetary relief" means the compensation which the magistrate may order the respondent to pay to the aggrieved person, at any stage during the hearing of an application seeking any relief under this Act, to meet the expenses incurred and the losses suffered by the aggrieved person as a result of the domestic violence;

Monetary relief is compensation payable to the aggrieved person to meet expenses incurred and losses suffered by aggrieved person as a result of domestic violence. Monetary relief can be granted by the magistrate at any stage of hearing of an application seeking any relief under this Act. The magistrate can only grant monetary relief if aggrieved person has been subjected to domestic violence. An aggrieved person does not need to initiate a separate proceedings for availing monetary reliefs. An aggrieved person can seek monetary relief in any pending proceeding seeking relief under the Act. Monetary reliefs can be sought by the aggrieved person under section 18 of the Act.

(l) "Notification" means a notification published in the official gazette and the expression "notified" shall be construed accordingly.

(m) "Prescribed" means prescribed by rules made under this Act;

(n) "Protection Officer" means an officer appointed by the State Government under sub-section (1) of section 8.

Protection officer is an important authority under the Act. Protection officer is appointed under sub-section (1) of Section 8. Protection officer functions as a bridge between aggrieved person, magistrate, police station, shelter home and service providers. Protection officer discharges various functions under the Act. Functions of protection officer includes preparing domestic incident report, assisting the aggrieved person in filing application under Section 12 of this Act, assisting aggrieved persons in getting police assistance, assisting aggrieved person in medical examination etc.

(o) "Protection Order" means an order made in terms of section 18.

(p) "Residence Order" means an order granted in terms of sub section (1) of Section 19;

(q) "Respondent" means any adult male person who is, or has been, in a domestic relationship with the aggrieved person and against whom the aggrieved person has sought any relief under this Act.

Provided that an aggrieved wife or female living in a relationship in the nature of a marriage may also file a complaint against a relative of the husband or the male partner.

As per this clause, the "respondent" is an adult male person who is or has been in a domestic relationship with the aggrieved person. In case of aggrieved wife or female living in relationship in the nature of marriage, she can file complaint against a relative of the husband or male partner. Thus in case of married wife or a female living in a relationship in nature of marriage, "Respondent" includes relative of the husband or the male partner. It can be seen the scope of "Respondent" is wider in case of married woman or a female living in a relationship in nature of marriage.

In *Varsha Kapoor vs. UOI & Others (2010)ILR 4 Delhi 383* mother-in-law of aggrieved has filed writ petition, wherein she has raised the ground *interalia* that only male relative of husband can be impleaded as "respondent". The Delhi High Court of Delhi dismissed the said writ petition and held that in case of aggrieved wife or female living in relationship of marriage, "respondent" will even include female relative of husband. Relevant para of the said judgment is as under:

> "*15. Having dissected definition into two parts, the rationale for including a female/woman under the expression 'relative of the husband or male partner' is not difficult to fathom. It is common knowledge that in case a wife is harassed by husband, other family members may also join husband in treating the wife cruelty and such family members would invariably include female relatives as well. If restricted interpretation is given, as contended by the petitioner, the very purpose for which this Act is enacted would be defeated. It would be very easy for the husband or other male members to frustrate the remedy by ensuring that the violence on the wife is perpetrated*

by female members. Even when Protection Order under Section 18 or Residence Order under Section 19 is passed, the same can easily be defeated by violating the said orders at the hands of the female relatives of the husband.

16. It is not even necessary to proceed on the aforesaid assumptions. Various provisions in the DV Act, provide for clinching the circumstances indicating that female relative was clearly in the mind of the legislature when it comes to filing of the complaint/ application by a wife or a female living in a relationship in the nature of marriage, as contemplated in proviso to Section 2(q). These provisions are Section 19, 21 and 31 of the DV Act. The wordings of Section 19 of the DV Act makes it clear that the section provides for disposal of applications made under subsection (1) of Section 12 by the Magistrate. Under Sub-section (1) of Section 19, the Magistrate can pass any order against a female person other than the orders under Clause (b). Whereas proviso to Sub-section (1) of Section 19 puts a bar on the power of the Magistrate for passing an order against any person who is a woman under Section 19(1)(b). In other words, except residence order under Section 19(1)(b), it is competent for the Magistrate to pass orders against the relatives of the husband including a female person under Section 19(1)(c) i.e., restraining the respondent or any of his relatives from entering any portion of the shared household in which the aggrieved person resides. For example, if the aggrieved person along with husband resides in a house owned by joint family including the presents of the respondent, his brothers and sisters, if any whether or not the respondent has no legal or equitable interest or title in the shared household, he can be restrained form dispossessing the aggrieved person. Further, under Sub-section (8) of Section 19, if am aggrieved person was provided with residential house towards her Stridhan, property or valuable security, namely, gold jewellery etc., which was in possession of the female member of the husband. Section 21 of the Act deals with grant of temporary custody of any child or children to the aggrieved person or the person making an application on her behalf and specifies necessary arrangements for visit of such child or children by the respondent. For instance, if the children are under the custody of mother-in-law of an aggrieved person, if we give arestricted meaning to Section 2(q), no such order can be passed for giving temporary custody of the child against a female relative of the husband, i.e., father, mother who are residing jointly."

Cielo

STRKING DOWN OF "ADULT MALE" BY THE SUPREME COURT

The definition of term "respondent" has been altered to a great extent as the term "adult male" has been struck down by the Supreme Court in **Hiral P. Harsora and Ors. vs. Kusum Narottamdas Harsora And Ors; (2016)10SCC165.** The Supreme Court has held that "adult male" discriminates between persons similarly situated and is contrary to objective sought to be achieved .The Court has held as under

> "*36. A conspectus of these judgments also leads to the result that the microscopic difference between male and female, adult and non adult, regard being had to the object sought to be achieved by the 2005 Act, is neither real or substantial nor does it have any rational relation to the object of the legislation. In fact, as per the principle settled in the **Subramanian Swamy** judgment, the words "adult person" person" are contrary to the object of affording protection to women who have suffered from "domesticviolence" of any kind". We, therefore, strike down the words"adult male" before the word "person" in Section 2(q), as these words discriminate between persons similarly situate, and far from being in tune with, are contrary to the object sought to be achieved by the 2005 Act.*"

The Hon'ble Court has further observed as under:

> "*40. An application of the aforesaid severability principle would make it clear that having struck down the expression "adult male" in Section 2(q) of the 2005 Act, the rest of the Act is left intact and can be enforced to achieve the object of the legislation without the offending words. Under Section 2(q) of the 2005 Act, while defining 'Respondent', a proviso is provided only to carve out an exception to a situation of "Respondent" not being an adult male. Once we strike down 'adult male', the proviso has no independent existence, having been rendered otiose.*"

The striking down of the word "adult male" by the Supreme Court has made the definition of "respondent" wider. Now a male as well as female can be a "respondent", if he/she has been in domestic relationship with aggrieved person. Further proviso of Section 2 (q), has also become redundant in light of striking down of "adult male".

(r)"service provider" means an entity registered under sub-section (1) of section 10;

(s) "shared household" means a household where the person aggrieved lives or at any stage has lived in a domestic relationship either singly or along with the respondent and includes such a household whether owned or tenanted either jointly by the aggrieved person and the respondent, owned or tenanted by either of them in respect of which either the aggrieved person or the respondent or both jointly or singly have any right, title, interest or equity and includes such a household which may belong to the joint family of which the respondent is a member, irrespective of whether the respondent or the aggrieved person has any right, title or interest in the share household.

The concept of shared household is important under the act as aggrieved person has been given right to reside in shared household, irrespective of whether she has any right, title or beneficial interest in the same.

As per this clause, shared household is a household where aggrieved person lives or at any stage has lived in a domestic relationship either singly or along with Respondent. Shared household includes such households owned and tenanted jointly by aggrieved person and the respondent; or owned or tenanted by either of them in respect of which aggrieved person and respondent both jointly or singly have any right, title, interest or equity. Shared household also includes households which may belong to joint family of which respondent is a member, irrespective of whether the respondent or the aggrieved person has any right, title or interest in the shared household.

It is pertinent to note that even such household, where an aggrieved person has lived singly, is covered in the definitions of shared household. The critical test is that such women should be in domestic relationship with the respondent.

The most distinguishing feature of the definition of shared household is the fact that right, title or interest of the aggrieved person over the shared household is immaterial for determination whether a household is shared household. Only two factors are relevant for determination whether a household is shared household. *Firstly*, there should exist domestic relationship between the aggrieved person and the respondent. *Secondly,* aggrieved person lives or at any stage has lived singly or jointly in the household.

It has been held by the Supreme Court in **S. R. Batra & ANR vs. Smt. Taruna Batra; (2007) 3 SCC 169** that an aggrieved person cannot claim every household to be shared household wherein she has lived with the respondent. Only those household can be covered under the definitions of shared household, where she has lived with husband or which is a joint family property. The Hon'ble Court has observed as under:

> "20. *If the aforesaid submission is accepted, then it will mean that wherever the husband and wife lived together in the past that property becomes a shared household. It is quite possible that the husband and wife may have lived together in dozens of places e.g. with the husband's father, husband's paternal grand parents, his maternal parents, uncles, aunts, brothers, sisters, nephews, nieces etc. If the interpretation canvassed by the learned Counsel for the respondent is accepted, all these houses of the husband's relatives will be shared households and the wife can well insist in living in the all these houses of her husband's relatives merely because she had stayed with her husband for some time in those houses in the past. Such a view would lead to chaos and would be absurd.*
>
> *It is well settled that any interpretation which leads to absurdity should not be accepted.*"

The Supreme Court in*Satish Chander Ahuja Vs. Sneha Ahuja (Civil Appeal 2483 of 2020)*has held that interpretation of shared household as put in S. R. Batra is not correct interpretation. The Court held that share household can not be limited to the house belonging to or taken on rent by the husband, or the house which belongs to the joint family of which the husband is a member. The respondent in a proceeding under the Act can be any relative of the husband. In event, the shared household belongs to any relative of the husband with whom in a domestic relationship the woman has lived, the conditions mentioned in Section 2(s) are satisfied and the said house will become a shared household. Relevant para is as under:

> "63. *The words "lives or at any stage has lived in a domestic relationship" have to be given its normal and purposeful meaning.*

The living of woman in a household has to refer to a living which has some permanency. Mere fleeting or casual living at different places shall not make a shared household. The intention of the parties and the nature of living including the nature of household have to be looked into to find out as to whether the parties intended to treat the premises as shared household or not. As noted above, Act 2005 was enacted to give a higher right in favour of woman. The Act, 2005 has been enacted to provide for more effective protection of the rights of the woman who are victims of violence of any kind occurring within the family. The Act has to be interpreted in a manner to effectuate the very purpose and object of the 62 Act. Section 2(s) read with Sections 17 and 19 of Act, 2005 grants an entitlement in favour of the woman of the right of residence under the shared household irrespective of her having any legal interest in the same or not.

64. In paragraph 29 of the judgment, this Court in S.R. Batra Vs. Taruna Batra (supra) held that wife is only entitled to claim a right to residence in a shared household and a shared household would only mean the house belonging to or taken on rent by the husband, or the house which belongs to the joint family of which the husband is a member. The definition of shared household as noticed in Section 2(s) does not indicate that a shared household shall be one which belongs to or taken on rent by the husband. We have noticed the definition of "respondent" under the Act. The respondent in a proceeding under Domestic Violence Act can be any relative of the husband. In event, the shared household belongs to any relative of the husband with whom in a domestic relationship the woman has lived, the conditions mentioned in Section 2(s) are satisfied and the said house will become a shared household. We are of the view that this court in S.R. Batra Vs. Taruna Batra (supra) although noticed the definition of shared household as given in Section 2(s) but did not advert to different parts of the definition which makes it clear that for a shared household there is no such requirement that the house may be owned singly or jointly by the husband or taken on rent by the husband. The observation of this Court in S.R. Batra Vs. Taruna Batra (supra) that definition of shared household in Section 2(s) is not very happily worded and it has to be interpreted, which is sensible and does not lead to chaos in the society also does not commend us. The definition of shared household is clear and exhaustive definition as observed by us. The object and purpose of the Act was to grant a right to aggrieved person, a woman of residence in shared household. The interpretation which is put by this Court in S.R. Batra Vs. Taruna Batra (supra) if accepted shall clearly frustrate the object and purpose of the Act. We, thus, are of the opinion that the interpretation of definition of shared household as put by this Court in S.R. Batra Vs. Taruna Batra (supra) is not correct interpretation and the said judgment does not lay down the correct law."

Cielo
JOINT FAMILY

Shared household includes a household belonging to joint family of which respondent is a member. Joint family has not been defined under the Act.

Delhi High Court in *Preeti Satija vs. Raj Kumari and Ors.; 207(2014)DLT78* has observed that joint status of family referred under the Act is in generic sense and equally applicable to all communities.

"21. Likewise, the interpretation preferred by some learned single judges that where the husband has some rights (as a member of the HUF, i.e. the Hindu Undivided Family) and if those premises were the shared household, the wife can enforce her right to residence, also constitutes an internally incoherent and restrictive interpretation of the Act. As explained in Evneet Singh, such a construction is contrary to Parliamentary intention that the law is a non-sectarian one. Indeed, the "joint" status of a family referred to under Section 2(s) is in a generic sense. To equate it with a HUF would result in unintended benefits to one set of respondents, who are Hindus. Speaking generically, "joint family" refers to a group of people, related either by blood or marriage, residing in the same house. Instances of that can be found in almost all parts of India. The general practice in India is that the son and his wife reside in the house of the (husband's) parents after marriage, though the legal obligation to maintain a child ceases as soon as she or he attains majority, the jural relationship between the parents and the child continues. The concept of a "joint family" in law is peculiar to Hindu law. No concept of a "joint family" similar to that of an HUF can be found in Muslim law, Christian law or any other personal law. Therefore, a restrictive

interpretation of "joint family" by equating it to a HUF would result in implicit discrimination, because women living in a shared household belonging to an HUF (and therefore, Hindus) would have more security, by reason of their professing the Hindu faith than others who are not Hindus. In fact, even among Hindus, women who are married into or live in HUFs, as compared with those living with husbands, whose parents own the property - on an application of Batra - would have the protection of the Act, while the latter would not. This inequity was addressed by the Parliament which stated in no uncertain terms that irrespective of title of the "Respondent" to the "shared household", a protection order can be made under Section 19(1)(a). "

Delhi High Court in *Navneet Arora vs. Surender Kaur; 213 (2014) DLT 611* has also taken a view that joint family is different than hindu undivided family.

"*76. Thus, it is unequivocally evinced from a perusal of the definitions enacted by various state legislatures in different enactments, that the term 'Joint Family' has a wider import than 'Hindu Undivided Family'; which stands subsumed therein*

77. The Gujarat High Court in its decision reported as 2012 Cri. L.J. 1187 Pritiben Jiteshbhai Upadhyay v. Jiteshbhai Virendrabhai Upadhyay & Ors., while dealing with a case under the Protection of Women from Domestic Violence Act, 2005, noticed the fact that the term 'Joint Family' was not defined under the Act and in order to assign a meaning to the same the Court cited with approval the definition comprised in Encyclopedia Britannica 2008. The same may be reproduced herein below:

"Joint family.-family in which members of a unilineal descent group (a group in which descent through either the female or the male line is emphasized) live together with their spouses and offspring in one homestead and under the authority of one of the members. The joint family is an extension of the nuclear family (parents and dependent children), and it typically grows when children of one sex do not leave their parents' home at marriage but bring their spouses to live with them. Thus, a patrilineal joint family might consist of an older man and his wife, his sons and unmarried daughters, his sons'

wives and children, and so forth. For a man in the middle generation, belonging to a joint family means joining his conjugal family to his family of orientation (i.e., into which he was born)."

78. We find that the meaning of the term 'Joint Family' for the purpose of Protection of Women from Domestic Violence Act, 2005 as approved by the Gujarat High Court contains no reference to 'Hindu Undivided Family'. "

(t) "shelter home" means any shelter home as may be notified by the State Government to be shelter home for purposes of this Act.

CHAPTER II

DOMESTIC VIOLENCE

This chapter covers defintion of "domestic violence". "Domestic violence" has been defined comprehensively under Section 3 of this Act.

3.Definition of domestic violence: For the purposes of this Act, any act, omission or commission or conduct of the Respondent shall constitute domestic violence in case it-

(a) harms or injures or endangers the health, safety, life, limb or well being, whether mental or physical, of the aggrieved person or tends to do so and includes causing physical abuse, sexual abuse, verbal and emotional abuse and economic abuse; or

(b) harasses, harms, injures or endangers the aggrieved person with a view to coerce her or any other person related to her to meet any unlawful demand for any dowry or other property or valuable security; or

(c)has the effect of threatening the aggrieved person or any person related to her by any conduct mentioned in clause (a) or clause (b); or

(d) otherwise injures or causes harm, whether physical or mental, to the aggrieved person.

Explanation I – For the purposes of this Section-

(i) "physical abuse" means any act or conduct which is of such a nature as to cause bodily pain , harm or danger to life, limb, or health or impair the health or development of the aggrieved person and includes assault, criminal intimidation and criminal force;

(ii) "Sexual abuse" includes any conduct of a sexual nature that abuses, humiliates, degrades, or otherwise violates the dignity of woman;

(iii) "Verbal and emotional abuse" includes-

(a) insults, ridicule, humiliation, name calling, and insults or ridicule specially with regard to not having a child or a male child; and

(b) repeated threats to cause physical pain to any person in whom the aggrieved person is interested.

(iv) "economic abuse" includes -

(a) deprivation of all or any economic or financial resources to which the aggrieved person is entitled under any law or custom whether payable under an order of a court or otherwise or which the aggrieved person requires out of necessity including , but not limited to household necessities for

the aggrieved person and her children, if any, stridhan, property, jointly or separately owned by the aggrieved person , payment of rental related to the shared household and maintenance. ;

(b) disposal of household effects, any alienation of assets whether movable or immovable, valuables, shares, securities, bonds and the like or other property, in which the aggrieved person has an interest or is entitled to use by virtue of the domestic relationship or which may be reasonably required by the aggrieved person or her children or her stridhan or any other property jointly or separately held by the aggrieved person, and

(c)Prohibition or restriction to continued access to resources and facilities which the aggrieved person is entitled to use or enjoy by virtue of the domestic relationship including access to the shared household.

Explanation II: For the purpose of determining whether any act, omission, commission, or conduct of the respondent constitutes "domestic violence" under this section, the overall facts and circumstances of the case shall be taken into consideration.

The definition of "domestic violence" is much wider than the definition of cruelty under the Indian Penal Code, 1860. The definition of "domestic violence" covers sexual abuse, economic abuse and emotional abuse which have not been covered under 498A of Indian Penal Code, 1860.

Clause (a) of Section 3 covers under definition of "domestic violence" act, omission, commission or conduct of the "respondent" which harms or injures or endangers the health, safety, life, limb or well being whether mental or physical. Domestic violence includes physical abuse, sexual abuse, verbal and emotional abuse and economic abuse. Physical abuse, sexual abuse, verbal and emotional abuse have been further defined in detail under the Explanation I.

Clause (b) of Section 3 covers under definition of domestic violence act, omission or conduct which harasses, harms, injures, or endanger to the aggrieved person with a view to coerce her or any other person related to her to meet any unlawful demand for any dowry or other property or valuable security.

Clause (c) of Section 3 covers under the definition of "domestic violence" the act, omission, commission or conduct of the respondent which has effect of threatening the aggrieved person or any person related to her by any conduct mentioned in clause (a) and (b).

Clause (d) is concerned with residual acts, omission, commission or conduct, which injures or causes harm, whether physical or mental to the aggrieved person.

From the perusal of the definition of the domestic violence, it emerges that only those incidences of violence have been covered, which a woman suffers within shared household by persons related by consanguinity, marriage or through a relationship in the nature of marriage, adoption or are family members living together as a joint family. The term domestic violence covers inter family affairs which are generally between immediate family members. It can not extend to family members who do not live under a shared household. The term "domestic violence" has to be understood in the context of "domestic relationship" and "shared household" and therefore, the relief sought for are meaningful only against the persons with whom the aggrieved person shares a domestic relationship and a shared household.

PHYSICAL ABUSE

It is a fundamental right of every citizen to enjoy life through his/her limb and faculty. There is widespread physical abuse of women in our society. Physical abuse can be in form of beating, slapping, hitting, biting, kicking, punching, pushing, shoving, causing bodily pain or injury in any other manner . There are various instances wherein husband after consuming alcohol indulges in physical abuse of wife which leads to bodily pain and endangers life, limb or health of women.

Physical abuse includes the following :

- Any act or conduct of the Respondent which causes bodily pain or harm
- Any act or conduct which causes danger to life, limb or health
- Any act or conduct of the Respondent which impairs the health or development of the aggrieved person
- Any act or conduct of the Respondent, which constitute assault, criminal intimidation and criminal force.

Physical abuse includes assault, criminal intimidation and criminal force. Criminal force has been defined under Section 350 of Indian Penal Code, 1860 as under:

350. Criminal Force: Whoever intentionally uses force to any person, without that person's consent, in order to committing of any offence, or intending by use of such force to cause , or knowing it to be likely that by use of such force he will cause injury, fear or annoyance to the person to whom the force is used, is said to use criminal force to that other.

Assault has been defined under Section 351 of Indian Penal Code as under:

351. Assault- Who ever makes any gesture or any preparation intending or knowing it to be likely that such gestures or preparation will cause any person present to apprehend that he who makes that gesture or preparation is about to use criminal force to that person, is said to commit an assault.

Explanation-Mere words do not amount to an assault. But the words which a person uses may give to his gestures or preparation such a meaning as may make those gestures or preparations amount to an assault.

Criminal Intimidation has been defined under Section 503 of Indian Penal Code as under:

503. Criminal Intimidation: Whoever threatens another with any injury to his person, reputation or property, or to the person or reputation of any one in whom that person is interested, with intent to cause alarm to that person, or to cause that person to do any act which he is not legally bound to do, or to omit to do any act which that person is legally entitled to do, as the means of avoiding the execution of such threat, commits criminal intimidation.

Explanation: A threat to injure the reputation of any deceased person in whom the person threatened is interested, is within this section.

SEXUAL ABUSE

A woman has fundamental right to be treated with dignity. Sexual abuse is one of the least reported form of doemstic violence. Sexual abuse has adverse physical, emotional and psychological effects on victims of domestic violence.

Sexual abuse has been defined as any conduct of a sexual nature that abuses, humiliates, degrades or otherwise violates the dignity of women.

Sexual violence can be in form of forced sexual intercourse, forcing aggrieved person to look at pornography or any other obscene pictures or material, any act of sexual nature to abuse, humiliate or degrade aggrieved person, or which is violative of dignity of aggrieved person or any other unwelcome conduct of sexual nature, child sexual abuse etc.

VERBAL AND EMOTIONAL ABUSE

Verbal and emotional abuse has also been covered under the defintion of domestic violence. Verbal an emotional abuse is another outcome of disadvantageous status of women in society. Married women are often verbally and emotionally abused. There was no remedy regarding this in Indian Penal Code, 1860. It is pertinent to mention here that insulting or ridiculing the aggrieved person with regard to not having a child or male child have been specially included due to unique social and cultural circumstances of the country, wherein a male child is preferred and sometimes a female/aggrieved person is insulted or ridiculed for not having a child.

Verbal and Emotional abuse includes the following:

- Insults, ridicule, humiliation and name calling
- Insults and ridicule specially with regard to not having a child or a male child
- Repeated threats to cause physical pain to any person in whom the aggrieved person is interested.

Verbal abuse can be in form of insults, name calling, accusations on character or conduct of aggrieved person, insults for not having a male child, insults for not bringing dowry, preventing aggrieved or a child in custody of aggrieved person from attending school, college or any educational institution, preventing aggrieved person from taking up a job, forcing aggrieved person to leave job, preventing aggrieved person or child in custody of aggrieved person for leaving the house, preventing aggrieved person from meeting any person in the normal course of events, forcing aggrieved person to get married when the aggrieved person does not want to marry, preventing aggrieved person from marrying a person of her own choice, forcing the aggrieved person to marry a particular person of his/their own choice, threatening the aggrieved person to commit suicide etc.

The definition of verbal and emotional abuse is not precise and words like ridicule and name calling are too general. Even a normal dispute between the aggrieved person and the respondent are sufficient to bring the matter in the Court. This has the potentiality of encouraging frivolous litigations.

ECOMONIC ABUSE

Although there have been reasonable economic empowerment of women in India, as yet majority of women are dependent on family members for their economic needs like food, cloths etc. Because of economic dependency, aggrieved woman are reluctant to report domestic violence incidents to police, court or any other public authority, as they are afraid that their survival will be at stake. Inclusion of economic abuse in the definition of domestic violence is definitely a progressive step as this can provide economic security to aggrieved women and will encourage aggrieved woman to report domestic violence incidents to appropriate authorities.

"Economic abuse" includes the following:

- Deprivation of economic and financial resources which aggrieved person is entitled under law and custom, which is payable either by order of court of otherwise.
- Deprivation of economic and financial resources which the aggrieved person requires out of necessity like household necessities for aggrieved person and her children, stridhan, property, jointly or separately by owned by the aggrieved person, payment of rental related to shared household and maintenance;
- Disposal of household effects
- Alienation of assets whether movable or immovable, valuables, shares, securities, bonds and the like
- Alienation of property in which the aggrieved person has an interest or is entitled to use by virtue of domestic relationship
- Alienation of property which may be reasonable required by the aggrieved person or her children
- Alienation of Stridhan
- Alienation of property jointly or separately held by the aggrieved person.
- Prohibition or restriction to continued access to resources
- Prohibition or restriction to facilities which the aggrieved person is entitled to use or enjoy by virtue of the domestic relationship including access to the shared house hold.

Economic violence can be in form of not providing the aggrieved person money for maintaining the aggrieved person or children, not providing food, cloths, medicine etc. to the aggrieved person or her children, stopping the aggrieved person from carrying on her employment, not allowing the aggrieved person to take up an employment, taking away income from salary, wages etc. of the aggrieved person, not allowing the aggrieved person to use her salary, wages etc, forcing the aggrieved person out of the house the aggrieved person lives in, stopping the aggrieved person from accessing or using any part of the house, not allowing use of clothes, articles or things of general household , not paying rent if staying in a rented accommodation etc.

High Court of Rajasthan in *Sabana (Smt.) @ Chand Bai and Anr. vs. Mohd. Talib and Anr; 2014(3)Crimes44(Raj.)* has observed on the scope of definition of "domestic violence" as under:

"33. Even a fleeting glimpse at Section 3 as reproduced above reflects that "domestic violence" has been widely defined and it covers within its ambit any act, omission or commission or conduct of the respondent resulting in physical, sexual, psychological and economic abuse or threat of such abuse being inflicted upon a woman who is or has been in domestic relationship with him. Undoubtedly, while the physical or sexual abuse caused by the respondent may be time specific, the emotional abuse caused cannot be time specific and its effects may persist even after the actual occurrence of the act of violence. Rather, the physical or sexual abuse may be the cause of subsequent psychological and emotional effects. Similarly, the "economic abuse" caused by depriving the aggrieved person from all or any economic and financial resources at any point of time or prohibiting or restricting the aggrieved person continued access to resources or facilities for which she is entitled will be in lot many cases a persisting domestic violence which cannot be restricted to a specific point in time and on that account the aggrieved person may be entitled to claim the reliefs under various provisions incorporated in the Act, pleading recurring cause of action. It is pertinent to note that as per Explanation I (iv), the deprivation of maintenance payable to the aggrieved person also falls within the definition of "economic abuse" for which the subsisting domestic relationship cannot be considered to be condition precedent for initiating the action inasmuch as even the divorced wife or the woman not in subsisting domestic relationship are also entitled for the maintenance

under the law."

The High Court of Patna in ***Chitranjan Prasad Singh vs. The State of Bihar and Ors.: I(2016)DMC197Pat.*** has observed on the scope of definition of domestic violence as under:

> "*20. The definition of 'domestic violence' suggests that it includes any act or conduct of the respondent, which causes harm, injury or endangers the health, safety, life, limb or to the wellbeing, whether mental or physical, of the aggrieved person, or even if the act or conduct of the respondent tends to do so and the definition further stipulates that such act or conduct includes causing physical, sexual, verbal, emotional or economic abuse. The definition also brings within its ambit, any conduct which harasses, harms, injures or endangers the aggrieved person, in order to coerce her or any other person related to her to meet any unlawful demand for any dowry or other property or valuable security. Even the act of threatening by any such conduct detailed above also gets covered by the definition of "domestic violence".*"

High Court of Bombay in ***XXX and Ors. vs. ABC and Ors. MANU/MH/ 0882/2016*** has observed has observed on the scope of definition of domestic violence as under:

> "*29. Thus, even a cursory glance to this definition of domestic violence is sufficient to know that it covers not only physical abuse, meaning thereby acts constituting danger to life, bodily pain, harm or something injurious to the health and development of a woman, but also covers insults, ridicule, humiliation, name calling, which are termed as verbal and emotional abuse. It also covers economic abuse, that of deprivation of all or any economic or financial resources. Thus, 'Domestic Violence' which is defined under this Act, is not limited to the physical harassment or physical violence but it also extends much beyond that and it is with an intention to secure her right to live with dignity, which is guaranteed under Article 21 of the Constitution of India, as fundamental right.*"

Cielo

Explanation II

As per explanation II, of this section , whether an act, omission and conduct of respondent will constitute domestic violence, overall facts and circumstances shall be taken into consideration. It seems that purpose of this explanation is to prevent undeserving complaints.

The High Court of Judicature of Bombay, in **Kishor vs. Shalini; 2010(112)BomLR1398** has observed as under:

> "*14. Perusal of the Explanation - II shows that the Court is required to take into consideration overall facts and circumstances.*
>
> *Explanation - II appears to have been inserted specifically with a view to enable the Court to find out the deserving and undeserving cases, which will be filed under the provisions of the Act of 2005. In the instant case the various factual aspects which I have noted above and in particular regarding the total eclipse for the period of 15 long years and in the absence of any complaint regarding domestic violence at any point of time before filing of the complaint in the recent past thereof or within reasonable period this Court is of the opinion that overall facts and circumstances of this case clearly show that even if the averments in the complaint are taken to be true at their face value, no case of domestic violence can even be inferred by the Court. The respondents could have adopted their remedy available under the other Laws for enhancement of maintenance or accommodation or rental or as the case may be, but certainly in the light of the above discussion the respondents were not entitled to take recourse to the Act of 2005. Consequently, the Court did not get jurisdiction under Section 27 of the Act of 2005 to entertain the complaint which was not maintainable for the above reasons. Both respondents, however, were entitled to take recourse to remedies under other Laws.*"

Cielo

DOMESTIC VIOLENCE PRECONDITION FOR RELIEF UNDER ACT

Suffering of domestic violence is precondition for granting of any relief under this Act. The Bombay High Court in **Mr. Prakash Kumar Singhee vs.**

Ms. Amrapali Singhee; 2018(2)Crimes333(Bom.) has observed as under:

"*12. Thus, in order to claim relief under Section 12 of the Act, which permits an "aggrieved person" to present an application to the magistrate seeking one or more reliefs under the Act, leveling allegations of Domestic Violence. Thus, the reliefs contemplated under the Act are thus available to an aggrieved person who alleges that she is or has been in domestic relationship with the respondent and was subjected to any Act of Domestic Violence by the Respondent. Allegation about the commission of a Domestic Violence is prerequisite for the magistrate or Court of competent jurisdiction to exercise the powers under the Protection of Women from Domestic Violence Act, 2005 and grant any reliefs contemplated under the Act*""

CHAPTER III

POWER AND DUTIES OF PROTECTION OFFICERS, SERVICE PROVIDERS ETC.

This chapter covers duties of protection officer, police officer, service providers, medical facilities and the government. The success of implementation of the Act depends upon these stakeholders.

4. Information to Protection Officer and exclusion of liability of informant:

(1) any person who has reason to believe that an act of domestic violence has been, or is being , or is likely to be committed, may give information about it to the concerned Protection Officer.

(2) No liability, civil or criminal, shall be incurred by any person for giving in good faith of information for purposes of sub-section (1).

Any person can inform the protection officer regarding act of domestic violence. Such person need not be aggrieved person. Such persons should have reasons to believe that act of domestic violence has been, or is being, or is likely to be committed.

The Act provides immunity from civil or criminal liability to persons informing the protection officer in good faith about acts of domestic violence.

Rule 4 of the Protection of Women from Domestic Violence Rules, 2006 provides procedure regarding information to protection officer. Rule 4 reads as under:

3. Information to Protection Officers- (1) Any person who has reason to believe that an act of domestic violence has been, or is being or is likely to be committed may give information about it to the Protection Officer having jurisdiction in the area either orally or in writing.

(2) In case the information is given to the Protection Officer under sub-rule (1) orally, he or she shall cause it to be reduced to in writing and shall ensure that the same is signed by the person giving such information and in case the informant is not in a position to furnish written information the Protection Officer shall satisfy and keep a record of the identity of the person giving such information.

46

As per Rule 4 , any person who has reason to believe that an act of domestic violence has been or is being or is likely to be committed may give information about it to the protection officer having jurisdiction in the area either orally or in writing. If the information is given orally to the protection officer, the protection officer has to get the information reduced to writing and get the information signed by the person who is giving the information. In case the informant is not in a position to furnish written information, the protection officer shall satisfy and keep a record of the identity of person giving such information.

5. Duties of police officers, service providers and Magistrate – A police officer, Protection Officer, service provider or Magistrate who has received a complaint of domestic violence or is otherwise present at the place of an incident of domestic violence or when the incident of domestic violence is reported to him, shall inform the aggrieved person-

(a) of her right to make an application for obtaining relief by way of protection order, an order for monetary relief, a custody order, a residence order, a compensation order or more than one such order under this Act;

(b) of the availability of services of service providers;

(c) of availability of services of the Protection Officers;

(d) of her right to free legal services under the Legal Services Authorities Act, 1987(39 of 1987)

(e)of her right to file a complaint under section 498A of the Indian Penal Code(45 of 1860) wherever relevant:

Provided that nothing in this Act shall be construed in any manner as to relieve a police officer from his duty to proceed in accordance with law upon a receipt of information as to the commission of a cognizable offence.

Legal literacy in India is not very high. An aggrieved person may not be always aware of her legal rights. It is needed that aggrieved person is informed about her legal rights under this Act and other legal provisions. The police officer, protection officer, service provider and the magistrate have been fastened with the duty to inform the aggrieved person of various reliefs available to her under various provisions of law, when such authorities receive complaint regarding incidence of domestic violence, or when such authorities are present at the place of incidence of domestic violence or domestic violence incidents are reported to them.

The aggrieved person has to be informed about her right to make application to the magistrate for obtaining reliefs by way of protection order, monetary order, custody order, residence order and compensation order under the Act. Aggrieved person has also to be informed about availability of services of service providers and protection officers.

Aggrieved person has, also, to be informed about her right to get free legal services under the Legal Services Authorities Act, 1987. Legal Services Authority Act, 1987 has been passed with the objective of providing free and competent legal services to weaker sections of society. Legal services are available to persons who fulfill criteria under Section 12 of the Legal Services Authority Act, 1987. Women are eligible for availing legal services under Section 12 of the Legal Services Authority Act, 1987. As per the section 2 (c) of Legal Services Act, 1987, "legal services" includes the rendering of any service in the conduct of any case or other legal proceedings before any court or other authority or tribunal and the giving of advice on any legal matter.

Aggrieved person has, also, to be informed of her right to file a complaint under section 498 A of the Indian Penal Code, 1860.

Further, this section does not relieve any police officer from his duty to proceed in accordance with law upon receipt of information as to the commission of a cognizable offence. This section does not dilute anyway remedies available to the aggrieved person against commission of cognizable offence. Cognizable offence has been defined under Section 2 (c) of Code of Criminal Procedure, 1973 as an offence for which, a police officer may, in accordance with the first schedule or under any other law for the time being in force, arrest without warrant.

6. Duties of shelter homes - If an aggrieved person or on her behalf a protection officer or a service provider requests the person in charge of shelter home to provide shelter to her, such person in charge of shelter home shall provide shelter to the aggrieved person in the shelter home.

Shelter homes provide safe accommodation to women who are victims of domestic violence. Shelter homes provide women protection, services and resources, which a victim of domestic violence needs on priority basis. Shelter home helps women in recovering from domestic violence, gaining self esteem and taking steps for independent life.

As per definition given under Section 2 (t) of the Act "shelter home" means any shelter home as may be notified by the State Government to be a shelter home for purposes of this Act. Section 6 casts a duty on the shelter home that if an aggrieved person or a protection officer on behalf of the aggrieved person or a service provider on behalf of the aggrieved person approaches shelter home and makes request to provide shelter to her, such person in charge of shelter home shall provide shelter to the aggrieved person.

Rule 16 of Protection of Women from Domestic Violence Rules, 2006 provides procedure for approaching shelter homes. Rule 16 of Protection of Women from Domestic Violence Rules, 2006. Rule 16 reads as under:

16. Shelter to the aggrieved person.--

(1) On a request being made by the aggrieved person, the Protection Officer or a service provider may make a request under section 6 to the person in charge of a shelter home in writing, clearly stating that the application is being made under section 6.

(2) When a Protection Officer makes a request referred to in sub-rule (1), it shall be accompanied by a copy of the domestic incident report registered, under section 9 or under section 10:

Provided that shelter home shall not refuse shelter to an aggrieved person under the Act, for her not having lodged a domestic incident report, prior to the making of request for shelter in the shelter home.

(3) If the aggrieved person so desires, the shelter home shall not disclose the identity of the aggrieved person in the shelter home or communicate the same to the person complained against.

As per Rule 16 of the Protection of Women from Domestic Violence Rules, 2006, if a request is made by the aggrieved person to the protection officer or service provider, such protection officer or service provider may make an application in writing under section 6 to the person in charge of the shelter home. If such application is made by protection officer, it shall be accompanied by domestic incident report.

It has also been provided in the Rule 16 of the Protection of Women from Domestic Violence Rules, 2006 that if aggrieved person desires that her identity is not disclosed then her identity shall not be disclosed by the shelter home or communicate the same to the person complained against.

7. Duties of medical facilities -If an aggrieved person or, on her behalf a protection officer or a service provider requests the person in charge of a medical facility to provide any medical aid to her, such person in charge of medical facility shall provide medical aid to the aggrieved person in the medical facility.

Victims of domestic violence suffer physical and psychological injury. Many of the victims of domestic violence need medical aid. State government have been authorized to notify medical facilities under Section 2 (j) of the Act.

Duty has been imposed on the medical facility that if an aggrieved person or protection officer on behalf of such aggrieved person or service provider on behalf of such aggrieved person approaches the medical facility and requests the person in charge of a medical facility to provide any medical aid to her, such medical facility has to provide medical aid to the aggrieved person.

Rule 17 of the Protection of Women from Domestic Violence Act, 2006 provides detail procedure for approaching the medical facility. Rule 17 reads as under:

17. Medical Facility to the aggrieved person.--

(1) The aggrieved person or the Protection Officer or the service provider may make a request under section 7 to a person in charge of a medical facility in writing, clearly stating that the application is being made under section 7.

(2) When a Protection Officer makes such a request, it shall be accompanied by a copy of the domestic incident report:

Provided that the medical facility shall not refuse medical assistance to an aggrieved under the Act, for her not having lodged a domestic incident report, prior to making a request for medical assistance or examination to the medical facility.

(3) If no domestic incident report has been made, the person-in-charge of the medical facility shall fill in Form I and forward the same to the local Protection Officer.

(4) The medical facility shall supply a copy of the medical examination report to the aggrieved person free of cost.

As per Rule 17 of the Protection of Women from Domestic Violence Rules, 2006, an aggrieved person can file application in writing under Section 7 of the Act to person in charge of the medical facility. Protection officer and service provider can also file such application on behalf of the aggrieved person. If such application is made by protection officer, it has to be accompanied by a copy of domestic incident report. Medical facility cannot refuse to grant medical assistance on the ground that no domestic incident report has been submitted. If no domestic incident report has been filed, medical facility has to fill Form I i.e. domestic incident report and forward the same to the protection officer. Medical facility has to provide a copy of examination report to the aggrieved person free of cost.

8. Appointment of Protection Officers: (1) The State Government shall, by notification, appoint such number of Protection Officers in each district as it may consider necessary and shall also notify the area or areas within which a Protection Officer shall exercise the powers and perform the duties conferred on him by or under this Act.

(2) The Protection Officer shall be as far as possible be women and shall possess such qualifications and experience as may be prescribed.

(3) The terms and conditions of service of the Protection Officer and the other officers subordinate to him shall be such as may be prescribed.

Under this Section, State Government has been empowered to appoint such number of Protection Officers as may be necessary and also notify their area of jurisdiction. Such protection officers as far as possible have to women. Qualification and experience of the protection officer has been prescribed by Protection of Women from Domestic Violence Rules, 2006. Rule 3 reads as under:

3. Qualifications and experience of Protection Officers.—

1. *The Protection Officers appointed by the State Government may be of the Government or members of non-governmental organizations: Provided that preference shall be given to women.*
2. *Every person appointed as Protection Officer under the Act shall have at least three years experience in social sector.*
3. *The tenure of a Protection Officer shall be a minimum period of three years.*
4. *The State Government shall provide necessary office assistance to the Protection Officer for the efficient discharge of his or her functions under the Act and these rules."*

The State Government can appoint any of its officer as protection officer. The State Government can also appoint any member of the non-government organization as protection officer. Women have to be given preference in appointment of protection officers. Any such person appointed as protection officer has to have at least 3 years experience in social sector.

Role of protection officer is critical to implementation of this Act. Despite that in many states adequate number of protection officers have not been appointed. Many of the protection officers are appointed on contractual basis and timely salary are not being paid to them. In such scenario protection officer will not be able to discharge their functions properly. The High Court of Gujarat has an occasion to consider the status of protection officers in **State of Gujarat in Suo Motu vs. State of Gujarat and Ors.; (2013)2GLR1047**. The High Court has observed as under:

"21. We have noticed having gone through the provisions of the Act that the Protection Officer plays an important role in proper implementation of the Act. Neither the Protection of Women from Domestic Violence Act, 2005 nor the Protection of Women from Domestic Violence Rules, 2006 permit the State Government to make any contractual appointments of Protection Officers for 11 months. In fact, Rule 3(3) says that the tenure of a Protection Officer shall be for a minimum period of three years. In our opinion, the contractual appointments of 11 months and less could be termed as contrary to the provisions of the Act. It is, therefore, imperative that the State Government completes the process of regular selection of Protection Officers for all districts in the State as early as possible. A Protection Officer has to be of a particular level and caliber. Having regard to the duties and functions of the Protection Officers, as provided in the provisions of the Act as well as the Rules, preference as provided in Rule 3 of Rules, 2006 should be given to the women and such person appointed as Protection Officer is expected to have at least three years experience in the social sector. In our opinion, it is only when a person is appointed as a Protection Officer on regular basis with regular salary that he would work with all sincerity and dedication.

22. We are also of the opinion that the State Government should have in place a proper system of man power planning to assess the needs of each district. For example, the materials on record indicate that districts like Ahmedabad, Jamnagar, Vadodara, Sabarkantha, Surat, Rajkot, Bhavnagar and Junagadh are the ones, where more than 100 applications in seven months have been received starting from January, 2011 till July, 2012. Conversely, districts like Navsari, Patan, Narmada, Surendranagar, Porbandar have received less than 25 applications in the period referred to above. Thus, in busy districts, one Protection Officer is simply not enough. To have one Protection Officer in a district like Ahmedabad, where more than 800 applications have been received in last 7 months, is nothing but a mockery of the Act. Therefore, the need of the hour is that the Government assess the needs of each district and accordingly, appoint adequate number of Protection Officers in each district to receive and attend the complaints in time.

23. We are also of the opinion that the State Government must ensure that the office of the District Social Defence Officer is provided with necessary staff and infrastructural facilities like furniture, computers, etc. This would only be in consonance with Rule 3(4) which provides that the State Government shall provide necessary office assistance to the Protection Officer for the efficient discharge of his or her functions and duties under the Act and the Rules.

24. The office of the Protection Officer is a statutory post. The Protection Officers under Sec. 30 of the Act are deemed to be Public servants. Therefore, like any other Government Servants, they should be entitled to pay-scale of appropriate rank with other allowances and service benefits as admissible to Government servants. The Act of 2005 being a benevolent piece of legislation and the Rules requiring preference to be given to women for appointments as Protection Officers, the State Government should ensure that labour turnover is not high in this area. One of the ways to ensure this, is to pay adequately to the Protection Officer. "

9. Duties and functions of Protection Officers- (1) It shall be duty of Protection Officer –

(a) to assist the Magistrate in the discharge of his functions under this Act;

(b) to make a domestic incident report to the Magistrate, in such form and in such manner as may be prescribed, upon receipt of a complaint of domestic violence and forward copies thereof to the police officer in charge of the Police Station within the local limits of whose jurisdiction domestic violence is alleged to have been committed and to the service providers in that area;

(c) To make an application in such form and in such manner as may be prescribed to the Magistrate , if the aggrieved person so desires, claiming relief for issuance of a protection order;

(d) To ensure that the aggrieved person is provided legal aid under the Legal Services Authority Act, 1987 (39 of 1987) and make available free of cost the prescribed form in which a complaint is to be made;

(e) to maintain a list of all service providers providing legal aid or counselling , shelter homes and medical facilities in a local area within the jurisdiction of the Magistrate;

(f) to make available a safe shelter home, if the aggrieved person so requires and forward a copy of his report of having lodged the aggrieved person in a shelter home to the police station and the Magistrate having jurisdiction in the area where the shelter home is situated;

(g) to get the aggrieved person medically examined ,if she has sustained bodily injuries and forward a copy of the medical report to the police station and the Magistrate having jurisdiction in the area where the domestic violence is alleged to have been taken place;

(h) to ensure that the order of monetary relief under section 20 is complied with and executed , in accordance with the procedure prescribed under the code of Criminal Procedure, 1973 (2 of 1974)

(i) to perform such other duties as may be prescribed.

(2) The protection officer shall be under the control and supervision of the Magistrate, and shall perform the duties imposed on him by the Magistrate and the Governement by, or under the Act.

Protection officer has been fastened with a number of duties under this Section and Rules 8,9 and 10 of Protection of Women from Domestic Violence Rules, 2006. Under this Section, the protection officer has been assigned following duties:

- The protection officer has to assist the magistrate in discharge of his functions
- The protection officer has to submit domestic incident report to the magistrate
- The protection officer has to make applications before the magistrate on behalf of aggrieved person
- The protection officer has to assist the aggrieved person in getting legal aid under the Legal Services Authority Act, 1987
- The protection officer has to maintain a list of service providers for providing legal aid and counseling services, shelter homes and medical facilities
- The protection officer has to make available safe shelter home to aggrieved person
- The protection officer has to get the aggrieved person medically examined if she has sustained bodily injuries

- The protection officer has to ensure that monetary relief granted under Section 20 of this Act is complied with
- The protection officer has to provide such other duties as may be prescribed.

DUTIES OF PROTECTION OFFICER UNDER RULE 8

Under Rule 8 of the Protection of Women from Domestic Violence Rules, 2006 certain duties have been imposed on the protection officer. Rule 8 reads as under:

Duties and function of Protection Officers - (1) It shall be the duty of the Protection Officer

(i) To assist the aggrieved person in making a complaint under the Act, if the aggrieved person so desires;

(ii) To provide her information on the rights of aggrieved persons under the Act as given in Form IV which shall be in English or in vernacular local language;

(iii) To assist the person in making any application under section 12 or subsection (2) of section 23 or any other provision of the Act or the rules made there under ;

(iv) To prepare a "Safety Plan" including measures to prevent further domestic violence to the aggrieved person, in consultation with the aggrieved person in Form V, after making an assessment to the dangers involved in the situation and on an application being moved under section 12;

(v) To provide legal aid to the aggrieved person , through the State Legal Services Authority;

(vi) To assist the aggrieved person and any child in obtaining medical aid at a medical facility including providing transportation to get the medical facility;

(vii) To assist in obtaining transportation for the aggrieved person and any child to the shelter;

(viii) To inform the service providers registered under the Act that their services may be required in the proceedings under the Act and to invite applications from service providers seeking particulars of their members to be appointed as Counsellors in proceedings under the Act under sub section (1) of Section 14 or Welfare Experts under Section 15;

(ix) To scrutinize the applications for appointment as Counsellors and forward a list of available Counsellors to the Magistrate;

(x) To revise once in three years the list of available counsellors by inviting fresh applications and forward a revised list of Counsellors on the basis thereof to the concerned Magistrate;

(xi) To maintain a record and copies of the report and documents forwarded under sections 9, 12, 20,21, 22, 23 or any other provisions of the Act or these rules;

(xii) To provide all possible assistance to the aggrieved person and the children to ensure that the aggrieved person is not victimized or pressurized as a consequence of reporting the incidence of domestic violence;

(xiii) To liaise between the aggrieved person or persons, police and service providers in the manner provided under the Act and these rules;

(xiv) To maintain proper records of the service providers, medical facility and shelter homes in the area of his jurisdiction.

(2) In addition to the duties and functions assigned to a Protection Officer under clauses (a) to (h) of subsection (1) of section 9, it shall be the duty of every protection officer –

(a) To protect the aggrieved person from domestic violence, in accordance with the provisions of the Act and these rules;

(b) To take all reasonable measures to prevent recurrence of domestic violence against the aggrieved person in accordance with the provisions of the Act and these rules.

Under the Rule 8 of the Protection of Women from Domestic Violence Act, 2006, following duties have been imposed upon the protection officer:

- The protection officer has to assist the aggrieved person in making a complaint under the Act
- The protection officer has to provide information to the aggrieved person about her rights as given in Form IV of the Act. Form IV of the Protection of Women from Domestic Violence Rules, 2006 consists of details of nature of domestic violence in form of physical violence, sexual violence, verbal and emotional violence, economic violence. It also has details of various reliefs under the Act including reliefs under section 18, 19, 20 and 22. It also has details of services provided by service providers.
- The protection officer has to assist the aggrieved person in making application under Section 12 or Sub-Section 2 of Section 23 or any

provision of the Act. Under Section 12 an aggrieved person or protection officer or any other person on behalf of the aggrieved person can present application for reliefs under the Act to the magistrate. Under Sub-Section 2 of Section 23, an aggrieved person can file application for ex parte order under Section 18, Section 19, Section 20, Section 21 or, as the case may be, Section 22.

- The protection officer has to prepare "Safety Plan" in Form V in consultation with the aggrieved person after making the assessment of dangers involved in the situation. Form V is an extensive form which consists of details about domestic violence i.e. physical abuse, verbal and emotional abuse, sexual abuse and economic abuse. It also consists of details regarding consequences of domestic violence faced by the aggrieved person. It also consists of details about apprehensions of the aggrieved persons.

- The protection officer has to provide legal aid to the aggrieved person through the State Legal Services Authority. State Legal Services Authority is an entity established under Section 6 of the Legal Services Authority Act, 1986 to provide free legal services to eligible persons Women are eligible to get legal services under the Legal Services Authority Act, 1986.

- The protection officer has to assist the aggrieved person and any child in getting medical aid at medical facility and to assist the aggrieved person in providing transportation to get medical facility.

- The protection officer has to assist in obtaining transportation for the aggrieved person and any child to shelter homes

- The protection officer has to inform the service providers for requirement of their services under the Act and to invite applications from service providers seeking particulars of their members to be appointed as counsellors under Section 14 or welfare expert under section 15. Under Section 14, the magistrate is empowered to direct the respondent or the aggrieved person, singly or jointly, to undergo counselling. Under Section 15, the Magistrate is empowered to secure the services of the welfare expert.

- The protection officer has to scrutinize the application for appointment as counsellors and forward a list of available counsellors to the magistrate.

- The protection officer has to revise once in three years the list of available counsellors by inviting fresh applications and forward a revised list of counsellors to the concerned magistrate.

- The protection officer has to maintain a record and copies of the report and documents forwarded under Section 9, 12, 20, 21, 22, 23 or any other provision of this Act or these rules.
- The protection officer has to provide all possible assistance to aggrieved person and children to ensure that the aggrieved person is not victimized or pressurized as a consequence of reporting the incidence of domestic violence.
- The protection officer has to liaise between the aggrieved persons or persons, police and service provider in the manner provided under the Act and these rules.
- The protection officer has to maintain proper records of service providers, medical facility and shelter homes in the area of his jurisdiction.

Additional duties have been assigned to the Protection Officer under sub-rule 2 of Rule 8 as under:

- The protection officer has to protect the aggrieved persons from domestic violence, in accordance with the Provisions of this Act and these rules.
- The protection officer has to take all reasonable measures to prevent recurrence of domestic violence against the aggrieved person, in accordance with the provisions of the Act and these rules.

DUTY OF PROTECTION OFFICER UNDER RULE 9

Rule 9 of the Protection of Women from Domestic Violence Rules, 2006 imposes certain duties upon the protection officer in cases of emergency. Rule 9 reads as under:

9. Action to be taken in cases of emergency- If the Protection Officer or a Service Provider receives reliable information through e-mail or a telephone call or the like either from the aggrieved person or from any person who has reason to believe that an act of domestic violence is being or is likely to be committed and in such an emergency situation, the Protection Officer or the Service Provider, as the case may be, shall seek immediate assistance of the Police who shall accompany the Protection Officer or the Service Provider, as the case may be, to the place of occurrence and record the domestic incident report and present the same to the Magistrate without any delay for seeking appropriate orders under the Act.

There are situations wherein urgent actions are required to address the incidents of domestic violence. Urgent actions have to be taken by protection officer and service providers in emergency situations under Rule 9 of Protection of Women from Domestic Violence Rules, 2006. If the protection officer or the service provider receives reliable information through e-mail or a telephone call or any other source either from aggrieved person or any person, protection officer or service provider has to seek immediate assistance of police. In such emergency situations, police is bound to accompany the protection officer or the service provider to place of occurrence of domestic violence. Protection officer has to record domestic incident report and without any delay has to forward the same to the magistrate for seeking appropriate orders under the Act.

DUTIES OF PROTECTION OFFICER UNDER RULE 10

One of the duties of the protection officer is to assist the magistrate under this Act. Certain duties in respect of assisting the magistrate have been provided under Rule 10 of the Protection of Women from Domestic Violence Rules, 2006. Rule 10 reads as under:

10. Certain other duties of the Protection Officers: (1) The Protection Officer, if directed to do so in writing , by the Magistrate shall-

(a) Conduct a home visit of the shared household premises and make preliminary inquiry if the Court requires clarification , in regard to granting ex parte interim relief to the aggrieved person under the Act and pass an order for such home visit;

(b) After making appropriate inquiry, file a report on the emoluments, assets, bank accounts, or any other documents as may be directed by the Court;

(c) Restore the possession of the personal effects including gifts and jewellery of the aggrieved person and the shared household to the aggrieved person;

(d) Assist the aggrieved person to regain custody of children and secure rights to visit them under his supervision as may be directed by the Court;

(e) Assist the court in enforcement of orders in the proceedings under the Act in the manner directed by the Magistrate ,including orders under

Section 12, Section 18, Section 19, Section 20, Section 21, or Section 23 in such manner as may be directed by the Court;

(f) Take the assistance of the Police, if required, in confiscating any weapon involved in the alleged domestic violence.

(2)The Protection Officer shall also perform such other duties as may be assigned to him by State Government or the Magistrate in giving effect to the provisions of the Act and these rules from time to time.

(3)The Magistrate may, in addition to the orders for effective relief in any case, also issue directions relating general practice for better handling of the cases to the protection officers within his jurisdiction and the Protection Officer shall be bound to carry out the same.

Under Section 10 of this Act, the protection officer has been assigned additional duties, which the protection officer can only do, if she has been directed to do so in writing by the magistrate. Such duties are as under:

- If the magistrate passes order for home visit in regard to *ex parte* interim relief, the protection officer has to visit shared household and make preliminary inquiry and after making preliminary inquiry file report on the emoluments, assets, bank accounts or any other documents as may be directed by the Court.
- If the magistrate directs, the protection officer has to restore the possession of the personal affects including gifts and jewellery of the aggrieved person and shared household to the aggrieved person.
- If the magistrate directs, the protection officer has to assist the aggrieved person to regain custody of children and secure rights to visit them under his supervision as may be directed by the Court.
- If the magistrate directs, the protection officer has to assist the Court in enforcement of orders in the proceedings under the Act in the manner directed by the magistrate, including orders under Section 12, Section 18, Section 19, Section 20, Section 21, or Section 23.
- If the magistrate directs, the protection officer has to take the assistance of the police, if required, in confiscating any weapon involved in the alleged domestic violence.

10. Service Providers- (1) Subject to such rules as may be made in this behalf, any voluntary association registered under the Societies Registration Act, 1860 (21 of 1860) or a company registered under the Companies Act, 1956 (1 of 1956) or any other law for the time being in force with the objective of protecting the rights and interests of women by any lawful means including providing of legal aid medical, financial or other assistance shall register itself with the State Government as a service provider for the purposes of this Act.

(2) A service provider registered under sub-section (1) shall have the power to-

(a) record the domestic incident report in the prescribed form if the aggrieved person so desires and forward a copy thereof to the Magistrate and the Protection Officer having jurisdiction in the area where the domestic violence took place;

(b) get the aggrieved person medically examined and forward a copy of the medical report to the Protection Officer and the Police Station within the local limits which the domestic violence took place.

(c) ensure that the aggrieved person is provided shelter in a shelter home, if she so requires and forward a report of the lodging of the aggrieved person in the shelter home to the police station within the local limits of which the domestic violence took place.

(3) No suit, prosecution or other legal proceedings shall lie against any service provider or any member of the service provider who is , or who is deemed to be , acting or purporting to act under this Act, for anything which is in good faith done or intended to be done in the exercise of powers of discharge of functions under this Act towards the prevention of the commission of domestic violence.

Domestic violence against women being a social, cultural and psychological issue, non-governmental orgnisations have been given important responsibilities under this Act. Non governmental orgnisations can register themselves as service providers and render various services under this Act. Service providers can provide services as counselling centre, welfare experts, shelter homes etc. Service providers have been empowered to prepare domestic incident report and forward the same to the magistrate and protection officer. Service provider can also get the aggrieved person medically examined and ensure that the aggrieved person is provided shelter in shelter home.

Any voluntary association registered under Society Registration Act, 1860 or any company registered under Companies Act, 1956 or any other law can register itself with state government as service provider. Such organization should have objective of protecting the rights and interests of women by any lawful means including providing of legal aid, medical, financial or other assistance.

The service providers and its members have been protected for anything done or intended to be done, which is in good faith in discharge of functions under this Act towards the prevention of the commission of domestic violence. No suit, prosecution and other legal proceedings can be instituted against any service provider or any member thereof for acts done under the Act in good faith

REGISTRATION OF SERVICE PROVIDER

Procedure of registration of service provider has been provided under rule 8 of Protection of Women from Domestic Violence Rules, 2006. The rule 11 reads as under:

11. Registration of service providers –

(1) Any voluntary association registered under the Societies Registration Act, 1860 (21 of 1860) or a company registered under the Companies Act, 1956 (1 of 1956) or any other law for time being in force with the objective of protecting the rights and interests of women by any lawful means including providing of legal aid, medical, financial or other assistance and desirous of providing service as a service provider under the Act shall make an application under sub-section (1) of section 10 for registration as service provider in Form VI to the State Government.

(2) The State Government shall, after making such enquiry as it may consider necessary and after satisfying itself about the suitability of the applicant, register it as a service provider and issue a certificate of such registration:

Provided that no such application shall be rejected without giving the applicant an opportunity of being heard.

(3) Every association or company seeking registration under sub-section (1) of section 10 shall possess the following eligibility criteria, namely:-

(a) It should have been rendering the kind of services it is offering under the Act for at least three years before the date of application for registration under the Apt and these rules as a service provider.

(b)In case an applicant for registration is running a medical facility, or a psychiatric counseling centre, or a vocational training institution, the State Government shall ensure that the applicant fulfils the requirements for running such a facility or institution laid down by the respective regulatory authorities regulating the respective professions or institutions.

(c) In case an applicant for registration is running a shelter home, the State Government shall, through an officer or any authority or agency authorized by it, inspect the shelter home, prepare a report and record its finding on the report, detailing that –

(i) the maximum capacity of such shelter home for intake of persons seeking shelter;

(ii) the place is secure for running a shelter home for women and that adequate security arrangements can be put in place for the shelter home;

(iii) the shelter home has a record of maintaining a functional telephone connection or other communication media for the use of the inmates;

(3) The State Government shall provide a list of service providers in the various localities to the concerned Protection Officers and also publish such list of newspapers or on its website.

(4) The Protection Officer shall maintain proper records by way of maintenance of registers duly indexed, containing the details of the service providers.

Under this rule, any voluntary association registered under the Societies Registration Act, 1860 or a company registered under Companies Act, 1956 or under any other law for the time being can apply to the State Government for registration as service provider in prescribed Form VI of this Act. Form VI consists of various details of service providers like name, address, service being rendered, persons being employed, duration of services etc. Form VI, also, consists of additional details like adequate space, area of premise, number of rooms, details of security arrangements, telephone connection, distance of nearest medical facility etc. in case of shelter homes. Form VI also consists additional details like number of counsellors, minimum qualification of counsellors, experience of counsellors, professional qualification of counsellors, types of counseling etc in case of counseling centres. The protection officer has to keep list of service providers under her jurisdiction.

The State Government may make an inquiry after receipt of application for registration as service providers. After making an inquiry and satisfying itself, State Government can register such organisations as service providers. State Government has also to issue a certificate of such registration. State Government cannot reject such application without granting the applicant an opportunity of being heard. Thus, State Government has to abide by the principles of natural justice before rejecting the application for registration.

ELIGIBILITY CRITERIA OF SERVICE PROVIDERS

Every voluntary association or company seeking to be registered with the State Government has to fulfill eligibility criteria as under.

- It should have at least three years of experience before the date of application in rendering services as it is offering under the Act or Protection of Women from Domestic Violence Rules, 2006
- If the application is for running a medical facility, or a psychiatric counseling centre or a vocational training institution, the State Government has to ensure that applicant fulfills the requirement of regulatory authorities in their respective fields.
- If the application is for running shelter homes, the State Government through appropriate officer inspect the shelter home and prepare a report. Such report has to record finding regarding (i) The maximum capacity of such shelter home for intake of persons seeking shelter, (ii) The place is secure for running shelter home for women and adequate security arrangement has been put, (iii) The shelter home has adequate arrangement for telephone connection or other communication media for the use of the inmates.

The State Government has to provide a list of service providers to protection officers and publish such list in the newspapers or on its website. The protection officer also has to maintain proper records of service providers by way of maintenance of registers duly indexed.

11. Duties of the Government: The central Government and every state government, shall take all measures to ensure that-

(a) The provisions of this Act are given wide publicity through public media including the television, radio, and the print media at regular intervals.

(b) the Central Government and State Government Officers including the police officers and the members of the judicial services are given periodic sensitization and awareness training on the issues addressed by this Act;

(c) effective co-ordination between the services provided by concerned Ministries and Departments dealing with law, home affairs including law and order, health and human resources to address issues of domestic violence is established and periodical review of the same is conducted;

(d) Protocols for the various ministries concerned with the delivery of services to women under this Act including the courts are prepared and put in place.

This Act is a social welfare legislation and it has to be given wide publicity by the Central Government and the State Government, so that people at large are aware of provisions of this Act. Sensitization of judicial officers, police officers, protection officers etc. is also essential for effective implementation of the Act. Domestic violence is not a purely legal issue, but it is also a social, cultural and psychological issue. Domestic violence can not be handled mechanically as law and order issue only. A proactive and sensitive approach has to be taken by judicial officers, police officers, protection officer,etc. for successful implementation of the Act.

Under Section 11 of the Act, the Central Government and the State Government has been directed to take all measures to ensure that all provisions of the Act are given wide publicity through public media including the television, radio, and print media at regular intervals. Wider publicity will help women and public at large in getting aware of their legal rights. Central Government and State Government have to ensure that Central Government Officers and State Government Officers including Police Officers and Judicial Officers are given periodic sensitization and awareness on issues addressed by the Act. Central and State Government have also to ensure that effective coordination between the services provided by concerned ministries and departments to address issues of domestic violence is established and periodical review of the same is conducted. Aforesaid initiatives on the part of the Government are essential for implementation of this Act in letter and spirit.

CHAPTER IV

PROCEDURE FOR OBTAINING ORDERS OR RELIEFS

This chapter covers procedure of filing of application for getting various reliefs under the Act, the nature of orders which can be granted by the magistrate, jurisdiction of the court of the magistrate, procedure of filing appeal against order of the Magistrate etc.

12. Application to Magistrate- (1) An aggrieved person or a Protection Officer or any other person on behalf of the aggrieved person may present an application to the Magistrate seeking one or more reliefs under this Act;

Provided that before passing any order on such application, the magistrate shall take into consideration any domestic incident report received by him from the Protection Officer or the service provider.

(2) The relief sought for under sub-section (1) may include a relief for issuance of an order for payment of compensation of damages without prejudice to the right of such person to institute a suit for compensation or damages for the injuries caused by the acts of domestic violence committed by the Respondent.

Provided that where a decree for any amount as compensation or damages has been passed by any court in favour of the aggrieved person, the amount, if any paid or payable in pursuance of the order made by the Magistrate under this Act shall be set off against the amount payable under such decree and the decree shall notwithstanding anything contained in the Code of Civil Procedure, 1908 (5 of 1908) or any other law for the time being in force, be executable for the balance amount , if any, left after such set off.

(3)Every application under sub-section (1) shall be in such form and contain such particulars as may be prescribed or as nearly as possible thereto.

(4)The magistrate shall fix the first date of hearing, which shall not ordinarily be beyond three days from the date of receipt of the application by the court.

(5)The Magistrate shall Endeavour to dispose of every application made under sub section (1) within a period of sixty days from the date of its first hearing.

This Section provides for procedure for filing application for availing reliefs under this Act. An Application under Section 12 of the Act can be filed by an aggrieved person or a protection officer or any other person on behalf of the aggrieved person before the magistrate. *Locus standi* to file complaint before the magistrate has been relaxed to the extent that even protection officer or any other person on behalf of the aggrieved person can file a complaint before the magistrate under the Act. Thus access to justice has been made easier for the aggrieved person. In such application, one or more reliefs available under the Act can be sought. Before passing an order on such application, the magistrate has to consider the domestic incident report filed by the protection officer or the service provider.

Under the application, the aggrieved person or a protection officer or any other person on behalf of the aggrieved person can also seek for payment of compensation or damages. Such relief does not in any way restricts the right of the aggrieved person to institute a suit for compensation or damages for the injuries caused by the acts of domestic violence committed by the respondent. It is pertinent to mention that this Act provides additional remedy and it does not disturb rights of aggrieved person to approach other forums.

If a decree for any amount as compensation or damages has been passed by any court in favour of an aggrieved person and an order is also passed by the magistrate for an amount to be paid to aggrieved person, such amount has to be set off against the amount payable under the decree. Balance amount, if any, is executable as decree, notwithstanding, anything, contained in the Code of Civil Procedure, 1908.

An application before the magistrate has to be made in prescribed form or as nearly as possible thereto. The magistrate has to fix the first date of hearing not beyond three days from date of receipt of application by the court.The magistrate has to make endeavour to dispose of every application within a period of sixty days from date of its first hearing. It seems that time line of 60 days is ambitious in light of huge number of pendency of cases before courts. Further this timeline of 60 days is only directory in nature and the magistrate is not bound to dispose of applications under 60 days.

Rule 6 of Protection of Women from Domestic Violence Rules, 2006 provides details of filing Application under Section 12 of the Act.

6. Application to the Magistrate – (1) Every Application of the aggrieved person under Section 12 shall be in form II or as nearly as possible thereto.

(2) An aggrieved person may seek the assistance of the Protection Officer in preparing her application under sub-rule (1) and forward the same to the concerned Magistrate.

(3) In case aggrieved person is illiterate, the Protection Officer shall read over the application and explain to her the contents thereof.

(4) The affidavit to be filed under sub-section (2) of the section 23 shall be filed in Form III.

(5)The Application under Section 12 shall be dealt with and orders enforced in the same manner laid down under Section 125 of the Code of Criminal Procedure, 1973.

As per Rule 6 every application under Section 12 has to be in Form II or as nearly as possible thereto. Form II, *inter alia,* consists of details of protection orders under Section 18, residence orders under Section 19, monetary reliefs under Section 20, custody order under Section 20 and compensation order under Section 22, which an aggrieved person may be seeking.

An aggrieved person may seek assistance of the protection officer in preparing her Application. If an aggrieved person is an illiterate person, the protection officer has to read over the application and explain its contents to the aggrieved person.

Under sub-section 2 of Section 23 of the Act, the magistrate has been empowered to pass *ex parte* orders against the respondent, if application prima facie discloses that the respondent is committing, or has committed an act of domestic violence or that there is a likelihood that the respondent may commit an act of domestic violence. But such *ex parte* orders can only be granted on the basis of an affidavit. Such affidavit has to be in Form III.

APPLICABILITY OF PROCEDURE UNDER SECTION 125 Cr.P.C. ON DOMESTIC VIOLENCE APPLICATION

As per Rule 6 (5) of the Protection of Women from Domestic Violence Rules, 2006, application under Section 12 has to be dealt with and orders enforced in the same manner as laid down under Section 125 of Code of Criminal Procedure. Applicant under Section 12 of this Act has not to be proceeded as regular complaint under the Code of Criminal Procedure, 1973. Section 125 of Code of Criminal Procedure, 1973 provides a summary proceedings to deal with applications filed thereunder. Bombay High Court in *Abhijit Bhikaseth Auti vs. State of Maharashtra and Ors. 2009CriLJ889* has observed as under :

> *"9. Form II of the said Rules incorporates a format of the application under Sub-section (1) of Section 12. The format requires that the nature of reliefs sought shall be incorporated in the application. Sub-rule (5) of Rule 6 provides that an application under*
>
> *Section 12 shall be dealt with and the orders passed thereon shall be enforced in the same manner laid down under Section 125 of the Code of Criminal Procedure, 1973 (hereinafter referred to as "the said Code"). The procedure which governs an application under Section 125 of the said Code will apply to the proceedings of an application under Section 12 of the said Act. The procedure contemplated by Chapter IX of the said Code which deals with applications under Section 125 is a summary procedure as indicated by Sub-section (2) of Section 126 of the said Code. Section 128 provides for enforcement of the order of maintenance. Thus, the orders passed by the learned Magistrate under the said Act are enforceable in the same manner as provided under Section 128 of the said Code."*

Cielo

DOMESTIC INCIDENT REPOERT NOT NECESSARY FOR ISSUING NOTICE

Majority of High Courts are of opinion that the magistrate is not bound to call for report of protection officer before issuing notice to respondents or passing orders. But if domestic incident report has been received by the magistrate then the magistrate is bound to consider the report of the Protection Officer.

In ***Bhupender Singh Mehra & Anr. vs. State of NCT of Delhi & Anr 2010(4)JCC2939*** the High Court of Delhi has taken a view that it was compulsory for magistrate to take into consideration domestic incident report submitted by the protection officer. The relevant portion of the said judgment is reproduced hereunder:

> *"5. An application under Section 12 of Domestic Violence Act has to be treated in accordance with provisions given under the Domestic Violence Act. Domestic Violence Act provides for obtaining domestic*

incident report. The domestic incident report proforma is given in form 1 of the schedule 2 of Domestic Violence Rules. This proforma is in detailed analytical form wherein the details of each incident of domestic violence are to be entered with date, time and place of violence and person who caused domestic violence. The purpose is that all allegations made in application must be specific and the Court should not exercise jurisdiction without considering domestic incident report since it is necessary for the Court to know before issuing any notice to respondent as to who was the respondent who caused domestic violence and what was the nature of violence and when it was committed. The proforma specifies different heads of physical violence, sexual violence, verbal and emotional abuse, economic violence, dowry related harassment and other forms of violence. The proforma also provides for filing of documents in support of the application like medico-legal certificate, list of istridhan and other documents. This domestic incident report has to be signed by the aggrieved person. The application under Section 12 is required to be made in form 2 of the Rules wherein the details of various kinds of reliefs and expenses are to be given. Section 27 of the Domestic Violence Act provides which judicial magistrate Court can have jurisdiction to entertain an application under Section 12 of the Act. Where marriage took place outside Delhi and the parties have lived outside Delhi, it is incumbent upon the applicant invoking jurisdiction of Delhi Court to specify how jurisdiction of Delhi Court was made out. No doubt Section 28(2) gives power to the MM of laying down its own procedure for disposal of an application under Section 12 or under Sub-Section 23(2) but the procedure an MM can adopt cannot be violative of the Act itself or violative of principles of natural justice. The procedure adopted by the learned MM of issuing notice to the respondent without even considering domestic incident report and without going through the contents of the application and without specifying as to why each of the respondent named by the applicant was to be summoned, is contrary to the Act. Only those persons can be summoned who have been in domestic relationship with aggrieved person. Under The Protection of Women from Domestic Violence Act, 2005 an aggrieved person does not have liberty to make every relative of the husband as a respondent. "*

High Court of Delhi in *Sambhu Prasad Singh vs. Manjri; 2013 (1) Crimes 414 (Del.)* after going through various provisions of the Act has held that magistrate is not bound to call for report of protection officer before issuing notice to respondents, but if domestic incident report has been placed on record, the same has to be considered by the magistrate.

> "13. The proviso to Section 12 obliges the court to, "before passing any order on such application... take into consideration any domestic incident report received by him from the Protection Officer or the service provider." The plenitude of the jurisdiction conferred by Section 12 is in no way affected by the proviso; all that it mandates is that before any order is made on an application (under Section 12) the magistrate "shall" take into consideration "any" report made by the Protection Officer. It is one thing to say that Parliamentary mandate to the court is to take into consideration, in every case, a protection Officers' report, as a precondition for exercise of jurisdiction - as the petitioner contends-and entirely another to say that if "any" such report is available, it shall be considered. This clear cut difference, in our opinion was lost sight of by the Single Judge in Bhupender Singh Mehra's case. If Parliament had indeed mandated that in every case the Court was obliged to call for a Protection Officer's report, and thereafter proceed with the complaint, the structure of Section 12 would have been entirely different. Such intention would have been expressed in more definitive, or imperative terms. In this context, this Court is also unpersuaded by the Petitioner's argument that Rule 6 and the form appended to the Rules have to be read into Section 12, to discern the precondition urged. This Court sees no need to do so; it would result in artificially curtailing what is otherwise a wide power."

The Hon'ble Court has further observed in the concluding paragraph as under:

> "18. To conclude we answer the question referred to the Court in the negative; a Magistrate, when Petitioned under Section 12 (1) is not obliged to call for and consider the DIR before issuing notice to the respondent. However, if the DIR has already been submitted, that should be considered, in view of the proviso to Section 12 (1). In view

of the fact that the Court has taken a view which results affirming the judgment of the Additional Sessions Judge as well as the concerned Metropolitan Magistrate (who had issued notice under Section 12 without calling for a report from the Protection Officer, and none was on the record) the petition is bereft of merit and it is therefore dismissed."

The *High Court of Punjab & Haryana in Eshan Joshi vs. Suman II(2018)CCR449(P&H)* has held that if no domestic incident report has been received by the court, then in such an eventuality there is no bar on the court to pass an order under Section 12 of this Act.

"19. In the case of Abhiram Gogoi v. Rashmi Rekha Gogoi (2011) 4 Gau LR 276, it was held by Hon'ble Gauhati High Court that it is not mandatory for a Magistrate to obtain a domestic incident report before the Magistrate passes a maintenance order under Section 18 of the DV Act. A similar view was taken by the Hon'ble Delhi High Court in the case of Shambhu Prasad Singh v. Manjari, 2012(3) R.C.R. (Criminal) 493, that receipt of domestic incident report is not a pre-requisite for issuing a notice to the respondent. Insistence to take into consideration the domestic incident report of protection officer would not apply at the stage of initiation of enquiry under Section 12 of the DV Act, because a Magistrate, on the basis of an application supported by affidavit, on being satisfied can even grant ex parte orders in favour of the aggrieved person under Sections 18, 19, 20, 21 or 22 of the DV Act. Even this High Court in the case Jag-dish Kumar Bakhri v. Manju Bakhri, 2012 SCC Online P&H 395, observed that a bare perusal of Section 12 of the DV Act would signify that it is not mandatory for the Court to call for domestic incident report on each and every date of hearing, before passing any order. If no domestic report is received in the court, then in such eventuality, there is no bar for the court to pass an order under Section 12 of the DV Act. The judgment relied upon by the counsel for the respondent in the case of Dharmendra and others v. State of M.P. and another, is contrary to the judgments referred to by this court. On a reading of the judgment, this court is not inclined to concur with the same."

The Supreme Court has also held in **Prabha Tyagi Vs. Kamlesh Devi (Criminal Appeal No. 511 of 2022)** that it is not mandatory for the magistrate to consider a domesic incident report. Magistrate can pass interim or final order even in absence of domestic incident report. Relevant para is as under:

> *"It is held that Section 12 does not make it mandatory for a Magistrate to consider a Domestic Incident Report filed by a Protection Officer or service provider before passing any order under the D.V. Act. It is clarified that even in the absence of a Domestic Incident Report, a Magistrate is empowered to pass both ex parte or interim as well as a final order under the provisions of the D.V. Act."*

Cielo

COMPLAINT MAINTAINABLE EVEN IF ACTS OF DOMESTIC VIOLENCE COMMITTED BEFORE COMING IN FORCE OF THE ACT

Even if acts of domestic violence has been committed before coming into force of this Act, and aggrieved person is no longer living with the respondent, the Complaint under Section 12 is maintainable. Delhi High Court in *Savita Bhanot vs. V. D. Bhanot; 2010(2)Crimes300* has observed as under:

> *"7. If the court takes the interpretation that a petition under the provisions of the Protection of Women from Domestic Violence Act, 2005 cannot be filed by a woman unless she was living with the respondent, in the shared household, on the date this Act came into force, or a date subsequent thereto or that a petition under the provisions of the Act cannot be filed by a person who has been subjected to domestic violence before coming into force of the Act, that would amount to giving a discriminatory treatment to the woman who despite living with the respondent and having a domestic relationship with him before coming into force of the Act, is later compelled to live separately from him on account of the acts attributable to the respondent and to the woman who was, prior to coming into force of the Act, subjected to domestic violence, viz a viz, the women who are living with the respondent or women in respect*

of whom acts of domestic violence are committed after coming into force of the act. There can be no reasonable classification based upon an intelligible differentia between the women who are living with the respondent on the date of coming into force of the Act or who are subjected to domestic violence after coming into force of the Act on one hand and the women who were living with the respondent or who were subjected to domestic violence prior to coming into force of the Act, on the other hand. Therefore, any discriminatory treatment to women in either category would be violative of their constitutional right guaranteed under Article 14 of the Constitution. The court needs to eschew from taking an interpretation which would not only be violative of the rights conferred upon the citizens under Article 14 of the Constitution but would also result in denying the benefit of the beneficial provisions of the Act to the women who have been subjected to domestic violence and are compelled to live separately from the respondent on account of his own acts of omission or commission. Such an interpretation would at least partly defeat the legislative intent behind enactment of the Protection of Women from Domestic Violence Act, 2005, which was to provide an efficient and expeditious civil remedy to them, in order either to protect them against occurrence of domestic violence, or to give them compensation and other suitable reliefs, in respect of the violence to which they have been subjected.

18. For the reasons given in the preceding paragraphs, I am of the considered view that a petition under the provisions of the Protection of Women from Domestic Violence Act, 2005 is maintainable even if the acts of domestic violence have been committed prior to coming into force of the Act or despite her having in the past lived together with the respondent a shared household woman is no more living with him, at the time of coming into force of the Act. It is be open for the Magistrate to pass appropriate order under the provisions of Sections 12, 18, 19, 20, 21, 22 or 23 of the Act on a petition filed by such a woman and the person who commits breach of the protection order or interim protection order passed on an application filed by such a woman will be liable to punishment under Section 31 of the Act."

The said view has been approved by the Supreme Court in **V. D. Bhanot vs. Savita Bhanot; (2012)3SCC183.**

"8. The attitude displayed by the Petitioner has once again thrown open the decision of the High Court for consideration. We agree with the view expressed by the High Court that in looking into a complaint under Section 12 of the PWD Act, 2005, the conduct of the parties even prior to the coming to force of the PWD Act, could be taken into consideration while passing an order under Sections 18, 19 and 20 thereof. In our view, the Delhi High Court has also rightly held that even if a wife, who had shared a household in the past, but was no longer doing so when the Act came into force, would still be entitled to the protection of the PWD Act, 2005."

In ***Juveria Abdul Majid Patni vs. Atif Iqbal Mansoori (2014) 10SCC736*** the Supreme Court has observed that if domestic violence has been committed subsequent decree of divorce shall will not absolve the respondent from the liability.

"30. An act of domestic violence once committed, subsequent decree of divorce will not absolve the liability of the respondent from the offence committed or to deny the benefit to which the aggrieved person is entitled under the Domestic Violence Act, 2005 including monetary relief under Section 20, child custody under Section 21, compensation under Section 22 and interim or ex parte order under Section 23 of the Domestic Violence Act, 2005."

MAINTAINABILITY OF SECTION 482 Cr.P.C PETITION AGAISNT ANY PROCEEDINGS UNDER THE ACT

Reliefs available under Sections 12, 18, 19, 20, 21, 22 and 23 are civil in nature. Exceptions are only Section 31, wherein breach of protection order has been made an offence and Section 33 wherein Protection Officer can be punished for not discharging duties. But the procedure adopted are that of Code of Criminal Procedure, 1973. Issues have arisen before courts whether the proceedings under the Act are criminal proceedings and whether Section 482 of Code of Criminal Procedure can be invoked to quash the proceedings initiated under the Act. Different High Courts have expressed different views on these issues.

High Court of Bombay in ***Mangesh Sawant vs. Minal Vijay Bhosale and Ors. 2012BomCR(Cri)458*** has held that power under Section 482 of Code of Criminal Procedure, 1973 can not be invoked for quashing the proceedings under Section 12 of the said Act in as the proceedings of the said application cannot be said to be criminal proceedings.

> *"9. Thus, the said Act cannot be said to a penal statute. Merely because the jurisdiction to entertain application under Section 12 has been conferred upon the learned Magistrate, the said Act cannot be termed as a penal statute and the proceedings under the said Act cannot be treated as Criminal proceedings. The power under the Act can be exercised even by a Civil Court or a Family Court.*
>
> *10. There is no question of the learned Magistrate taking cognizance of a complaint under Section 12 of the said Act. There is no provision for issuing a summons contemplated by Code of Criminal Procedure, 1973 on the application under Section 12. Therefore, power under Section 482 of the said Code cannot be invoked for quashing the proceedings of application under Section 12 of the said Act in as much as the proceeding of the said application cannot be said to be a criminal proceeding. In any case, it is well settled law that the power under Section 482 can be exercised sparingly and in only exceptional cases."*

A larger bench of Bombay High Court in **Nandkishor Pralhad Vyawahare vs. Mangala 2018(1)BomCR(Cri)449** has over ruled the view taken in **Mangesh Sawant vs. Minal Vijay Bhosale and Ors. 2012BomCR(Cri)458.** The larger bench has taken a view that proceedings under Protection of Women from Domestic Violence Act, 2005 is predominantly civil in nature but Section 482 Cr.P.C. can be invoked for quashing the same.

> *"56. In the case of Sukumar Gandhi (supra), the Division Bench of this Court, however, held that because the proceedings under Section 12(1) initiated to obtain various reliefs under the Act, mainly being of civil nature, no resort to Section 482 of Cr.P.C. could be taken for the purpose of seeking their quashment. It was of the view that if such an inference is made, it would defeat the very object of the D.V. Act of providing for a speedy and effective remedy for enforcing an amalgamation of civil rights. Accordingly, it held that barring the prosecutions initiated for trying of the offences prescribed under the Act, inherent power of the High Court under Section 482 of Cr.P.C. could not be invoked for quashing of the proceedings. In view of the*

discussion made and the conclusions drawn in the earlier paragraphs, it is not possible for us to agree with the view so taken by the Division Bench of this Court and we declare it to be an incorrect view. If we accept the opinion of the Division Bench, the result, in our view, would be quite opposite to what has been thought of by it. That apart, making Section 482 of Cr.P.C. as not applicable may also amount to doing harm to plain and clear language of Section 28 of the D.V. Act, which expresses unequivocally and clearly the intention of the Parliament, thereby excluding the possibility of resorting to external aids and other rules of construction.

57. While there is no difference of opinion about what the intention of the Parliament is, our disagreement is with the view that this very intention gets defeated by applying the provision of Section 482 to the proceedings under Section 12(1) of the D.V. Act and it is achieved by removing its applicability. The issue can be examined from a different angle as well.

58. A plain reading of Section 482 of Cr.P.C., which saves inherent power of the High Court, indicates that the power is to be exercised by the High Court not just to quash the proceedings, rather it has to be exercised for specific as well as broader purposes. The exercise of the inherent power has been delimited to such purposes as giving effect to any order under the Code or to prevent abuse of the process of any Court or otherwise to secure the ends of justice. This would show that the inherent power of the High Court can be invoked not only to seek quashing of a proceeding, but also to give effect to any order under the Code or to challenge any order of the Court, which amounts to abuse of the process of the Court or generally to secure the ends of justice. This would mean that not only the respondent-man but also the aggrieved person-woman may feel like approaching the High Court to give effect to any order or to prevent abuse of the process of Court or to secure ends of justice. This would show that this power is capable of being used by either of the parties and not just by the respondent seeking quashing of the proceedings under Section 12 of the D.V. Act. If this power is removed from Section 28 of the D.V. Act, the affected woman may as well or equally get adversely hit, and this is how, the very object of the D.V. Act may get defeated.

59. Now, one incidental question would arise as to from what stage the provisions of the Cr.P.C. would become applicable and in our view, the answer could be found out from the provisions of Sections 12 and 13 of the D.V. Act. A combined reading of these provisions shows that the commencement of the proceedings would take place the moment, the Magistrate applies his mind to the contents of the application and passes any judicial order including that of issuance of notice. Once, the proceeding commences, the procedure under Section 28 of the D.V. Act, subject to the exceptions provided in the Act and the rules framed thereunder, would apply. In other words, save as otherwise provided in the D.V. Act and the rules framed thereunder and subject to the provisions of sub-section (2) of Section 28, the provisions of the Cr.P.C. shall govern the proceedings under Sections 12 to 23 and also those relating to an offence under Section 31 of the D.V. Act on their commencement. "

Gujarat High Court in **Narendrakumar vs. State of Gujarat (2014)2GLR1353)** had held that mere use of the provisions of Cr.P.C. for limited purposes of Secs. 12, 18 to 23 and 31 of D.V. Act would not ipso facto attract Sec. 482 of Cr.P.C.:

"14.1. From the scheme of D.V. Act, as aforementioned, the emphasis on 'aggrieved person', 'domestic violence', 'domestic incident report' is eloquent. As per Sec. 12, aggrieved person or protection officer or any other person on behalf of the aggrieved person is entitled to move an application, and as noticed in Sec. 2(a), 'aggrieved person" is a woman in domestic relationship with 'respondent' alleging a commission of domestic violence by such respondent. Thus, the application under Sec. 12 can be moved by or on behalf of a woman suffering from domestic violence. Thus the 'domestic violence' is only the cause of action for reliefs under Secs. 17 to 23 of the D.V. Act.

14.2. Further, the provisions are also made for establishment of various facilitators like shelter homes, service providers, protection officers to assist the Magistrate and aggrieved person as also to enhance her knowledge about rights available to her under D.V. Act or I.P.C. or Dowry Prohibition Act. Thus, the remedies contemplated under D.V. Act except the one under Sec. 31 are not remedies under criminal law. Domestic violence may confer a cause upon the aggrieved person to proceed against the 'respondent' under criminal law and or under D.V. Act. Therefore, though the expression 'violence' connotes criminality referable to criminal mindset, the object of act being to assist the aggrieved person suffering from domestic violence by providing to her various reliefs as above and the act of domestic violence not being punishable under D.V. Act, it cannot be said that mere use of expression 'violence' would render the applications under Secs. 12, 17 to 24 of the D.V. Act as criminal proceedings. The fact that the civil remedies are provided to aggrieved person is also made eloquent by Objects and Reasons of D.V. Act as well.

14.3. True that the object of Sec. 31 is to punish the offender for violation of protection orders issued under Sec. 18 of D.V. Act. Breach of protection orders is classified as cognizable and non-bailable offence under Sec. 32, and upon testimony of the aggrieved person, the Court may conclude that offence under sub-sec. (1) of Sec. 31 has been committed by the accused. Protection order can be issued under Sec. 16 and its breach is cognizable under Sec. 32. The purpose of Secs. 31 and 32 appears to be to ensure compliance of protection orders, if necessary, by enforcing a 'criminal machinery against the offender. It is only while hearing a case under Sec. 31 that a charge can be framed also under Sec. 498A of I.P.C. or any other provision of that Code or the Dowry Prohibition Act, as the case may be, on disclosure of the commission of an offence under those provisions. Pertinently, except in relation to few provisions like Secs. 5 and 31, there is no reference to the expression 'offence', 'crime' or the like in entire D.V. Act. Therefore, even by virtue of doctrine of exclusion, an inference that none of the commissions or omissions except those made specifically punishable, the D.V. Act not intended to punish the 'respondent'.

14.4. For the foregoing reasons, it cannot be said that the acts or omissions constituting 'domestic violence' as defined in Sec. 3 of D.V. Act constitute an offence under D.V. Act so as to attract Sec. 4(2) of Cr.P.C.

14.5. In contrast, in order to attract Sec. 4(2) of Cr.P.C., the commissions or omissions complained of must necessarily be an offence as defined in Sec. 2(n) of Cr.P.C. Reference to various terms as quoted in Para 13.1 of this judgment as also the constitution of various Courts to try offences; the procedure to investigate or inquire into the offences; obligations cast upon the police or others for prevention and detection of offences; provisions for maintenance of public order and tranquility etc., all go to indicate that predominant object of Cr.P.C. is to provide for the procedure to deal with offences. Since the scheme of Cr.P.C. predominantly prescribes a procedure to try offences, Sec. 482 of Cr.P.C. also can be applied in relation to offences and not in relation to civil proceedings.

14.6. The procedure contemplated under Sec. 28 of D.V. Act applying the Criminal Procedure Code to the proceedings under Secs. 12, 18 to 23 and 31 of D.V. Act would not ipso facto attract Sec. 482 of Cr.P.C. Having regard to the scheme of D.V. Act, Sec. 28 while adopting the provision of Cr.P.C. intends to apply procedure necessary for passing orders for securing the civil rights contemplated under Secs. 12, 18 to 23 of D.V. Act. To illustrate, a Magistrate may issue the summon or warrant for securing the presence of 'respondent' as defined in Sec. 2(q) of the D.V. Act. Pertinently, Sec. 28, while referring to various provisions of D.V. Act prefixes the expression 'offence' to Sec. 31 only thus making the intent of the act very specific and eloquent. In other words, the expression 'offence' is prefixed to Sec. 31 as referred to in Sec. 28, while the said expression is omitted in Sec. 28 in reference to other provisions of D.V. Act, because Sec. 31 declares the breach of protection order an offence and other provisions do not. Further, under the very provision, Magistrate is empowered to prescribe its own procedure as well in which event the Magistrate may not have to rely upon Cr.P.C.

14.7. Thus, mere use of the provisions of Cr.P.C. for limited purposes of Secs. 12, 18 to 23 and 31 of D.V. Act would not ipso facto attract Sec. 482 of Cr.P.C.

14.8. Further, 'domestic violence‘ as defined in Sec. 3 of the Act has attributes of crime inasmuch as such acts may constitute an offence under one or other provisions of I.P.C. The Magistrate is one of the authorities contemplated under Cr.P.C. to deal with offences. It appears, that keeping the above aspect in view, it was deemed appropriate to authorise a judicial mind well-versed with the procedure dealing with crime, also to deal with the proceedings arising under D.V. Act since criminal acts as defined under Sec. 3 of D.V. Act give rise to cause of action under that Act. Furthermore, in case of breach of protection orders, the Magistrate is empowered to proceed under Sec. 31 of D.V. Act and also to frame charge for the offence under Sec. 498A of I.P.C. Therefore also it appears that the Magistrate has been selected as competent judicial authority to deal with the proceedings arising under D.V. Act and the Court of Sessions is contemplated as competent appellate authority. Thus, merely because judicial authorities contemplated under Cr.P.C. are found competent to deal with the proceedings arising under D.V. Act, it cannot be argued that such proceedings deal with crime.

15. The decision relied upon by learned Counsel for the petitioners in Inderjit Singh Grewal (supra) does not address the question as above. It merely invokes Sec. 468 of Cr.P.C. in a case arising under D.V. Act. Therefore, cannot be cited as an authority laying down the proposition of law discussed by this Court as above."

High Court of Gujarat in **Suo Motu Vs. Ushaben Kishorbhai Mistry: 2016ALLMR (Cri)293 of 2015** has held that prior of initiation of proceedings under Section 12 or 18 or 19 or 20 or 21 or 22 or 23 or 31 of the Act, any affected person may file Application under Artilce 226 of the Constitution. Once initiation of proceedings under Section 12 or 18 or 19 or 20 or 21 or 22 or 23 or 31 of the Act, either independently or jointly on account of any judicial order passed by the learned magistrate including issuance of notice, such proceedings shall be governed by the Code of Criminal Procedure and remedies under criminal procedure will be available including remedy under Section 482 of Code of Criminal Procedure, 1973.

"27. In view of the aforesaid observations and discussion, the following conclusions:

(i) The provisions of the Act provide for remedial measures for civil rights of women but the machinery provided is through criminal court.

(ii) Initiation of proceedings under Section 12 or 18 or 19 or 20 or 21 or 22 or 23 or 31 of the Act would begin only when the Magistrate has passed any judicial order including of issuance of notice for hearing.

(iii) Any person affected by any proceedings under the Act, prior to initiation of proceedings under Section 12 of the Act may prefer Special Criminal Application under Article 226 of the Constitution if as per him, the proceedings are beyond the scope and ambit of the Act or without any authority in law. But this Court, while entertaining the petition under Article 226 of the Constitution may decline entertainment of the petition by way of self-imposed restriction in exercise of the judicial powers or may decline entertainment of the petition in exercise of its sound judicial discretion.

(iv) Once proceedings are initiated under Section 12 or 18 or 19 or 20 or 21 or 22 or 23 or 31 either independently or jointly on account of any judicial order passed by the learned Magistrate including issuance of notice, such proceedings shall be governed by the Code of Criminal Procedure coupled with the power of the Court under Section 28(2) to lay down its own procedure for disposal of an application under Section 12 or under sub-section (2) of Section 23 of the Act.

(v) Once the applicability of the Code of Criminal Procedure has started on account of any judicial order passed by the learned Magistrate including issuance of notice either under Section 12 or 18 or 19 or 20 or 21 or 22 or 23 or 31 of the Act independently or jointly, remedial measures to the aggrieved person as provided under the Code of Criminal Procedure, 1973 can be said as available. But the higher forum under the Code of Criminal Procedure, may be the Court of Session or the High Court, may decline entertainment of such proceedings considering the facts and circumstances of the case and as per the settled principles of law and in accordance with law.

(vi) The aforesaid remedial measures provided under the Code of Criminal Procedure would also include the powers of this Court under Section 482 of the Code, but the Court may, in a given case, decline entertainment of the petition when there is express remedy provided under the Code of Criminal Procedure or no case is made out to prevent the abuse of process of any Court, or no case is made out to secure the ends of justice. "

Cielo

DOMESTIC VIOLENCE APPLICATION CAN BE AMENDED

An Application under Section 12 of the Act can be amended. The Court is not powerless to allow amendment of application under Section 12 of the Act. The Supreme Court in *K unapareddy@Nookala Shanka Balaji vs. Kunapareddy Swarna Kumari; (2016) 11 SCC 774* has observed as under:

"18. What we are emphasizing is that even in criminal cases governed by the Code, the Court is not powerless and may allow amendment in appropriate cases. One of the circumstances where such an amendment is to be allowed is to avoid the multiplicity of the proceedings. The argument of the learned Counsel for the Appellant, therefore, that there is no power of amendment has to be negated.

19. In this context, provisions of Sub-section (2) of Section 28 of the DV Act gain significance. Whereas proceedings under certain Sections of the DV Act as specified in Sub-section (1) of Section 28 are to be governed by the Code, the Legislature at the same time incorporated the provisions like Sub-section (2) as well which empowers the Court to lay down its own procedure for disposal of the application Under Section 12 or Section 23(2) of the DV Act. This provision has been incorporated by the Legislature keeping a definite purpose in mind. Under Section 12, an application can be made to a Magistrate by an aggrieved person or a Protection Officer or any other person on behalf of the aggrieved person to claim one or more reliefs under the said Act. Section 23 deals with the power of the Magistrate to grant interim and ex-parte orders and Sub-section (2) of Section 23 is a special provision carved out in this behalf which is as follows:

(2). If the Magistrate is satisfied that an application prima facie discloses that the Respondent is committing, or has committed an act of domestic violence or that there is a likelihood that the Respondent may commit an act of domestic violence, he may grant an ex parte order on the basis of the affidavit in such form, as may be prescribed, of the aggrieved person Under Section 18, Section 19, Section 20, Section 21 or, as the case may be, Section 22 against the Respondent.

20. The reliefs that can be granted by the final order or an by interim order, have already been pointed out above wherein it is noticed that most of these reliefs are of civil nature. If the power to amend the complaint/application etc. is not read into the aforesaid provision, the very purpose which the Act attempts to sub-serve itself may be defeated in many cases."

Cielo

APPLICABILITY OF LIMITATION ON DOMESTIC VIOLENCE APPLICATION

This Act does not prescribe any limitation period for filing of application under Section 12. Procedure under the Act is governed by Code of Criminal Procedure, 1973. Issues have arisen before the Court whether limitation period as prescribed under Section 468 of the Code of Criminal Procedure, 1973 is applicable or provisions of Limitation Act, 1963 are applicable on an Application filed under Section 12 of this Act.

The Supreme Court in **Inderjit Singh Grewal vs.State of Punjab and Ors. (2011)12SCC588** has held that provisions of Section 468 of Code of Criminal Procedure, 1973 is applicable on Applications under Section 12 of the Protection of Women from Domestic Violence Act, 2005.

> "*24. Submissions made by Shri Ranjit Kumar on the issue of limitation, in view of the provisions of Section 468 Code of Criminal Procedure, that the complaint could be filed only within a period of one year from the date of the incident seem to be preponderous in view of the provisions of Sections 28 and 32 of the Act 2005 read with Rule 15(6) of The Protection of Women from Domestic Violence Rules, 2006 which make the provisions of Code of Criminal Procedure applicable and stand fortified by the judgments of this Court in Japani Sahoo v. Chandra Sekhar Mohanty AIR 2007 SC 2762; and Noida Entrepreneurs Association v. Noida and Ors. (2011) 6 SCC 508.*"

The Supreme Court in **Krishna Bhatacharjee vs Sarathi Choudhury And Anr; (2016) 2 SCC 705** has held that limitation will not apply to domestic violence cases, which are in nature of continuing offences.

> "*31. Regard being had to the aforesaid statement of law, we have to see whether retention of stridhan by the husband or any other family members is a continuing offence or not. There can be no dispute that*

wife can file a suit for realization of the stridhan but it does not debar her to lodge a criminal complaint for criminal breach of trust. We must state that was the situation before the 2005 Act came into force. In the 2005 Act, the definition of "aggrieved person" clearly postulates about the status of any woman who has been subjected to domestic violence as defined under Section 3 of the said Act.

"Economic abuse" as it has been defined in Section 3(iv) of the said Act has a large canvass. Section 12, relevant portion of which have been reproduced hereinbefore, provides for procedure for obtaining orders of reliefs. It has been held in Inderjit Singh Grewal (supra) that Section 498 of the Code of Criminal Procedure applies to the said case under the 2005 Act as envisaged under Sections 28 and 32 of the said Act read with Rule 15(6) of the Protection of Women from Domestic Violence Rules, 2006. We need not advert to the same as we are of the considered opinion that as long as the status of the aggrieved person remains and stridhan remains in the custody of the husband, the wife can always put forth her claim under Section 12 of the 2005 Act.

We are disposed to think so as the status between the parties is not severed because of the decree of dissolution of marriage. The concept of "continuing offence" gets attracted from the date of deprivation of stridhan, for neither the husband nor any other family members can have any right over the stridhan and they remain the custodians. For the purpose of the 2005 Act, she can submit an application to the Protection Officer for one or more of the reliefs under the 2005 Act. In the present case, the wife had submitted the application on 22.05.2010 and the said authority had forwarded the same on 01.06.2010.

In the application, the wife had mentioned that the husband had stopped payment of monthly maintenance from January 2010 and, therefore, she had been compelled to file the application for stridhan. Regard being had to the said concept of "continuing offence" and the demands made, we are disposed to think that the application was not barred by limitation and the courts below as well as the High Court had fallen into a grave error by dismissing the application being barred by limitation."

The Hyderabad High Court in *J. Shyam Babu vs. State of Telangana 2017(4)Crimes332(A.P.)* has held after extensively analyzing the provisions of this Act and Code of Criminal Procedure, 1973 that limitation prescribed under Section 468 is not applicable to proceedings for getting relief under Section 18 to Section 23 of this Act. Section 468 of the Code of Criminal Procedure, 1973 is only applicable in case of nonpayment of compensation awarded or for non-implementation of the orders passed under Sections 12, 18 to 23 of the Act, which tantamount to offence.

"30. Once such is the case and these aspects when not covered in any expression rendered earlier either by this court or of the Apex Court, the same is hit by sub-silentio including the expression of this court in Cri. P. No. 8935 of 2014 and the expression of the Apex Court in Inderjit Singh Grewal v. State of Punjab & another in Cri. A. No. 1635 of 2011 and it is not the case where that by referring all these provisions it was held by interpreting compensation as part of the fine or as one of the modes of sentence and thereby the limitation is applicable. This conclusion on the principle of sub-silentio can be taken aid from the expression of the Division Bench of this Court in Gadda Balaiah v. The Joint Collector, Ranga Reddy District which quoted with approval the expressions of the Apex Court in Municipal Corporation of Delhi v. Gurnam Kaur and A One Granites v. State of U.P. that a judgment sub-silentio is not law declared within the meaning of Article 141 of the Constitution of India. Accordingly and in the result, it is made clear by holding that to initiate proceedings and to take cognizance for the reliefs to be claimed outcome of domestic relationship under Sections 12 r/w 18 to 23 of the Act, the question of application of period of limitation under Chapter XXXVI of the Code does not arise and the same have no application but for from what in the Act provided in case of nonpayment of compensation awarded or for non-implementation of the orders passed under Sections 12, 18 to 23 of the Act, to enforce the same for such violation which tantamounts to an offence to cognizance of which the period of limitation provided by Chapter XXXVI of the Code arises and not otherwise. Having regard to the above all the contentions raised in the revision are groundless and the Criminal Revision Case is thereby dismissed. No order as to costs."

Madras High Court in *M.G.M.Joseph Anand vs Suvitha Suganthi Crl (OP(MD)Nos.10110 & 15734 of 2011)* has also held that limitation provided under Section 468 of the Code of Criminal Procedure is not applicable to the application filed under Section 12 of this Act. But Section 468 comes into play when cognizance of offence is sought under Section 31 or 33 of the Protection of Women from Domestic Violence Act, 2005.

"10.It is true that Section 28 of the Central Act 43 of 2005 states that all proceedings under Section 12of the Protection of Women from Domestic Violence Act, 2005 shall be governed by the provisions of Code of Criminal Procedure, 1973. Therefore, applicability of Cr.PC to a proceeding initiated under Section 12 of the D.V act 2005 cannot be in doubt. But, now the question is whether Section 468 of Cr.PC can be said to apply to a petition filed under Section 12 of the D.V Act, 2005. Section 468 of Cr.PC engrafts a bar to taking cognizance after lapse of the period of limitation. Chapter 36 of Cr.PCwhich includes Section 467 to 473 bears the title "Limitation for taking cognizance of certain offences". Therefore, this Chapter and particularly Section 468 of Cr.PC cannot have any bearing or applicability in respect of proceedings which do not deal with taking cognizance of offences.

11.Section 31 of the Central Act 43 of 2005 prescribes penalty for breach of protection order by the respondent. Section 33 embodies penalty for not discharging duty by Protection Officer. Therefore, Section 468 of Cr.PC will come into play when cognizance is sought to be taken in respect of offences set out under the Protection of Women from Domestic Violence Act, 2005. When a person aggrieved seeks certain reliefs under provisions such as 12, 18, 19, 20, 21 and 22 etc., she does not call upon the court concerned to take cognizance of any offence committed by the opposite party. She only wants certain reliefs to be ordered in her favour. Therefore, respectfully following the later decision of the Hon'ble Supreme Court reported in (2016) 2 SCC 705 (Krishna Bhattarchargee vs. Sarathi Choudhury), I hold that Section 468 of Cr.PC does not apply to a petition filed under Section 12 of the Prevention of Women from Domestic Violence Act, 2005. Hence, the contention raised by the learned Senior Counsel appearing for the petitioner deserves to be negatived."

The Gujarat High Court in *T. Armstrong Changsan vs. Neikol Changsan; 2018(2)GLT411* has held that general law of limitation will apply to an application under Section 12 of this Act.

> *"37. When the domestic violence per-se is not made punishable under the D.V. Act nor violation of all orders under the D.V. Act is made punishable; except the offence as contemplated in Section 31 & 33 of the Act. Therefore, applicability of Section 468 Cr.P.C. in case of D.V. Act shall be limited only in case of offences under Section 31 & 33 of the D.V. Act and the said provision of Section 468 Cr.P.C. cannot be invoked in case of filing an application under Section 12 of the D.V. Act for any relief under Section 18, 19, 20, 21 or 22.*
>
> *38. However, from the ratio laid down by the Apex Court that concept of continuing offence gets attracted to domestic violence, it can be held as corollary that law of limitation shall apply to an application under Section 12 of the D.V. Act, though Section 468 Cr.P.C. may not be made applicable in case of filing an application under Section 12 of D.V. Act, having regard to the scheme and object of the act and the relief prescribed under various provisions of the D.V. Act as well as the scope of the provisions of Section 468 of the Cr.P.C. Needless to say, that when application under Section 12 of D.V. Act is filed seeking relief under the D.V. Act alleging domestic violence, which from the nature of violence attracts the concept of continuing offence, the same necessarily shall be governed by the concept of continuing offence, so far the starting point of limitation is concerned. When the provision of limitation as provided by Section 468 of the Cr.P.C. is limited to the offence only, necessarily question will arise, what shall be the period of limitation for filing an application under Section 12 of the D.V. Act which does not deal with any offence under the D.V. Act. Having regard to the object and scheme of the Act, this court is of the view that general law of limitation i.e. Limitation Act shall apply to an application under Section 12 of the D.V. Act."*

13. (1) A notice of the date of hearing fixed under section 12 shall be given by the Magistrate to the Protection Officer, who shall be given by the Magistrate to the Protection Officer, who shall get it served by such means as may be prescribed on the respondent, and on any other person,

as directed by the Magistrate within maximum period of two days or such further reasonable time as may be allowed by the Magistrate from the date of the receipt.

(2) A declaration of service of notice made by the Protection Officer in such form as may be prescribed shall be the proof that such notice was served upon the respondent and on any other person as directed by the Magistrate unless the contrary is proved.

A notice of application under section 12 has to be served to the respondents through protection officer. Such notice has to be served within two days or such reasonable time as may be allowed by the magistrate.

Rule 12 of Protection of Women from Domestic Violence Rules, 2006 provides detail procedure of serving notice to the Respondents.

"*12. Means of service of notices- (1) The notice for appearance in respect of the proceedings under the Act shall contain the names of persons alleged to have committed domestic violence, the nature of domestic violence and such other details which may facilitate the identification of person concerned.*

(2) The service of notices shall be made in the following manner, namely:-

(a) The notices in respect of the proceedings under the Act shall be served by the Protection Officer or any other person directed by him to serve the notice, on behalf of the protection officer, at the address where the respondent is stated to be ordinarily residing in India by the complainant or aggrieved person or where the respondent is gainfully employed by the complainant or the aggrieved person as the case may be.

(b) The notice shall be delivered to any person in charge of such place at the moment and in case of such delivery not being possible it shall be pasted at a conspicuous place on the premises.

(c) For serving the notices under Section 13 or any other Provision of the Act, the provisions under Chapter VI of the Code of Criminal Procedure, 1973 (2 of 1974) as far as practicable may be adopted.

(d)Any order passed for such service of notices shall entail the same consequences, as an order passed under Order V of the Civil Procedure Code, 1908(5 of 1908) or Chapter VI of the Code of Criminal Procedure, 1973 (2 of 1974) respectively, depending upon

the procedure found efficacious for making an order for such service under section 13 or any other provision of the Act and in addition to the procedure prescribed under the Order V or Chapter VI, the Court may direct any other steps necessary with a view to expediting the proceedings to adhere to the time limit provided in the Act.

(3) On a statement on the date fixed for appearance of the respondent , or a report of the person authorized to serve the notices under the Act, that service has been affected appropriate orders shall be passed by the Court on any pending application for interim relief, after hearing the complainant or the respondent or both.

(4) When a protection order is passed restraining the respondent from entering the shared household or the respondent is ordered to stay away or not to contact the Petitioner, no action of the aggrieved person including an invitation by the aggrieved person shall be considered as waiving the restraint imposed on the respondent, by the order of the Court unless such protection order is duly modified in accordance with provisions of sub-section (20 of Section 25. "

The notice for appearance has to contain names of persons who have been alleged to commit domestic violence and nature of domestic violence. Such notice has to have details of nature of domestic violence also.

Notices have to served through protection officer or any other person directed by Protection Officer on behalf of protection officer. Such notices have to served where the respondent is residing or where the respondent is gainfully employed. The notice has to be delivered to any person in charge of such place at the moment and in case such delivery is not possible, the notice has to be pasted at a conspicuous place on the premises.

While serving the notice, the provisions of Order V of the Civil Procedure Code 1908 or Provisions under Chapter VI of the Code of Criminal Procedure as far as practicable may be adopted. Any order passed for such service of notices shall entail the same consequences, as the order passed under Order V of the Civil Procedure Code, 1908 or Chapter VI of the Code of Criminal Procedure, 1973 respectively. The Court may direct any other steps necessary with a view to expediting the proceedings to adhere to the time limit provided in the act.

Thus magistrate has a wide discretion over the procedure to be adopted to serve notice on the respondent. The magistrate can issue notice as per procedure provided under the Code of Civil Procedure or Code of Criminal

Procedure. Only determining factor is practicability and efficaciousness of such step.

Patna High Court in **Manish Kumar Soni and Ors. vs. The State of Bihar and Ors. 2016(4)Crimes236(Pat.)** has observed that service of notice on an application filed under Section 12 or interim relief under Section 23, must be in the manner provided under the Code of Civil Procedure

> "*15. Section 13 of the Act which is under Chapter IV of the Act provides the mode of service of notice, which stipulates that notice will be given by the Magistrate to the Protection Officer who shall get it served by such means as may be prescribed on the respondent, and on any other person, as directed by the Magistrate within a maximum period of two days or such further reasonable time as may be allowed by the Magistrate from the date of its receipt.*
>
> *16. Sub-section (2) of Section 13 stipulates that any declaration of service of notice made by the Protection Officer in such form as may be prescribed shall be the proof that such notice was served upon the respondent and on any other person as directed by the Magistrate unless the contrary is proved. Hence, Section 13 provides that notice of the date of hearing fixed under Section 12 shall be given by the Magistrate to the Protection Officer, who shall get it served by such means as may be prescribed, on the respondent and on any other person, within a maximum period of two days or such further reasonable time as may be allowed by the Magistrate.*
>
> *17. It appears from the record that the application under Section 12 of the Act was filed by O.P. No. 2 on 25.11.2013 in the court of the learned Chief Judicial Magistrate, Vaishali at Hajipur, when the matter was transferred under Section 192 Cr.P.C., to the Court of the learned S.D.J.M. On 28.11.2013 the applicant was examined on S.A. by the learned S.D.J.M. and report was called for, from the District Protection Office, Vaishali, as to whether any complaint alleging torture has been filed earlier or not. On 12.12.2013 the enquiry witness was examined. The learned S.D.J.M. vide order dated 20.12.2013 directed for issuance of notice to the petitioners through the Project Manager-cum-District Woman Rights Protection Officer. The order dated 03.01.2014 reflects that reminders were directed to be issued for service of notice since the opposite parties did not appear after service of notice and the matter was adjourned for*

10.01.2014 when the report was submitted by the Project Manager-cum-District Woman Rights Protection Officer to the effect that in spite of valid service of notice, the Opposite parties failed to appear. Thereafter, the matter was adjourned for 13.01.2014 and vide order dated 18.01.2014 it was recorded to the effect that in spite of service of notice, the opposite parties are not appearing. On 22.01.2014 only one witness C.W. No. 1 Priyanka Kumari, Project Manager-cum-District Woman Rights Protection Officer was examined and on request of O.P. No. 2 evidence was closed and the matter was posted for ex-parte hearing.

18. Though Rule 12 of the Rules provides the means of service of notice. Sub-rule (1) of Rule 12 of the Rules does not specifically prescribe that notice is to be issued to the person concerned in Form VII, but when Section 13(1) is read along with Form VII, it can only be construed that the notice provided under Rule 12(1) should be in Form VII. If so, the Magistrates, before whom application under Section 12 of the Act are filed, are required to issue notices to the person alleged to have committed domestic violence, in Form VII as prescribed under the Rules. It is pertinent to note that the Form VII notice directs the person concerned to appear either personally or through a duly authorized counsel to show cause why the reliefs claimed against him shall not be granted and on the failure to appear that court shall ultimately proceed ex-parte against him. Clause (c) of Sub-rule (2) of Rule 12, makes it clear that for serving notices under Section 13 or any other provision of the Act, the provisions of Order V of the Code of Civil Procedure or the provisions under Chapter VI of the Code of Criminal Procedure, as far as practicable may be adopted.

19. As is clear from the Statement of Objects and Reasons, the Protection of Women from Domestic Violence Act is enacted to provide for a remedy under the civil law, which is intended to protect the women from being the victims of domestic violence and to prevent the occurrence of domestic violence in the society. Therefore, essentially the reliefs provided under the Act are civil remedies. The penal provisions are only Sections 31 and 33. Therefore, service of notice on an application filed under Section 12 or interim relief under Section 23, must be in the manner provided under the Code of Civil Procedure. "

Notice under Section 12 of this Act is different than summon under Section 61 of Code of Criminal Procedure, 1973. Magistrate can not issue summon under Section 12 of the Act. Only if a protection order is passed and the same is not complied with, it will constitute offence, and then only summon can be issued to the Respondent. The Madras High Court in *Sowdammal vs Meena MANU/TN/3085/2017* has observed as under:

> "*9. A mere reading of* <u>Section 13</u>*of the said Act would amply make the point clear that at the initial stage, the Magistrate was not justified in treating the respondents in this case as accused and as such, hereafter relating to applications under* <u>Section 12</u> *of the Protection of Women from* <u>Domestic Violence Act</u>, *the Magistrate should not issue summons under* <u>Section 61</u> *Cr.P.C. treating the respondents as accused. What is contemplated under* <u>Section 13</u> *of the Act is a notice specifying the date etc., The endeavour should be on the part of the officer concerned is to deal with the matter gently and treating the respondents in a gentle manner and that should not be lost sight of. Unless the appearance of the respondents are absolutely necessary on a particular date, they should not be simply harassed by compelling them to appear as though they are offenders. The Magistrate should not lose sight of the fact that so long as the case is anterior to the protection order being passed, they should be treated only as respondents. However, after the order under* <u>Section 18</u> *of the Act is passed and if there is violation, then the proceedings might get changed and become criminal proceedings. As such, the Magistrates hereafter would scrupulously adhere to the mandates contained in the Act itself.*"

14. Counselling- (1) The magistrate may, at any stage of the proceedings under this Act, direct the Respondent or the aggrieved person , either singly or jointly, to undergo counselling with any member of a service provider who possess such qualifications and experience in counselling as may be prescribed.

(2) When the Magistrate has issued any direction under sub-section (1), he shall fix the next date of hearing of the case within a period not exceeding two months.

Domestic violence is a social, cultural and psychological issue. Victims of domestic violence need help of professional counsellors for taking informed decision. Section 14 of the Act empowers the magistrate to direct the respondent or the aggrieved person at any stage of proceedings to undergo counselling with any member of service provider. Such service provider should possess relevant prescribed qualification and experience. The magistrate can direct respondent and aggrieved person to undergo counseling singly or jointly. The magistrate has to fix next date of hearing within a period not exceeding two months.

Rule 13 of Protection of Women from Domestic Violence Rules, 2006 provides details about appointment of counsellors:

13. Appointment of Counsellors.--

(1) A person from the list of available Counsellors forwarded by the Protection Officer, shall be appointed as a Counsellor, under intimation to the aggrieved person.

(2) The following persons shall not be eligible to be appointed as Counsellors in any proceedings, namely:-

(i) any person who is interested or connected with the subject matter of the dispute or is related to any one of the parties or to those who represent them unless such objection is waived by all the parties in writing.

(ii) any legal practitioner who has appeared for the respondent in the case or any other suit or proceedings connected therewith.

(3) The Counsellors shall as far as possible be women.

As per Rule 13, a counsellor has to be appointed by magistrate from the list of cousellors provided by protection officer. Rule 13 further provides details that who cannot be appointed as counsellor under the Act. A person who is interested or connected with subject matter of the dispute or related to one of the parties cannot be appointed as cousellors. But if such objections are waived by the parties in writing, even a person who is interested or connected with subject matter of the dispute or related to one of the parties can be appointed as cousellors. A legal practitioner who has appeared for the respondent in the case or any other suit or proceedings connected therewith cannot be appointed a as cousellor. It is pertinent to mention that only legal practitioners who have represented the respondent in the case or any other suit or proceedings connected therewith have been barred to be appointed as cousellor. A legal practitioner who has represented the applicant in the case or suit or proceedings connected therewith is competent to be appointed as cousellor. Rule 13 also provides that cousellors shall, as far as, possible be women.

Detailed procedure of counselling has been provided under Rule 14 of the Protection of Women from Domestic Violence Rules, 2006 as under.

14. Procedure to be followed by Counsellors.--

(1) The Counsellor shall work under the general supervision of the court or the Protection Officer or both:

(2) The Counsellor shall convene a meeting at a place convenient to the aggrieved person or both the parties.

(3) The factors warranting counselling shall include the factor that the respondent shall furnish an undertaking that he would refrain from causing such domestic violence as complained by the complainant and in appropriate cases an undertaking that he will not try to meet, or communicate in any manner through letter or telephone, electronic mail or through any medium except in the counselling proceedings before the counsellor or as permissibly by law or order of a court of competent jurisdiction.

(4) The Counsellor shall conduct the counseling proceedings bearing in mind that that the counseling shall be in the nature of getting an assurance, that the incidence of domestic violence shall not get repeated.

(5) The respondent shall not be allowed to plead any counter justification for the alleged act of domestic violence in counseling the fact that and any justification for the act of domestic violence by the respondent is not allowed to be a part of the Counselling proceeding should be made known to the respondent, before the proceedings begin.

(6) The respondent shall furnish an undertaking to the Counsellor that he would refrain from causing such domestic violence as complained by the aggrieved person and in appropriate cases an undertaking that he will not try to meet, or communicate in any manner through letter or telephone, e-mail, or through any other medium except in the counseling proceedings before the Counsellor.

(7) If the aggrieved person so desires, the Counsellor shall make efforts of arriving at a settlement of the matter.

(8) The limited scope of the efforts of the Counsellor shall be to arrive at the understanding of the grievances of the aggrieved person and the best possible redressal of her grievances and the efforts shall be to focus on evolving remedies or measures for such redressal.

(9) The Counsellor shall strive to arrive at a settlement of the dispute by suggesting measures for redressal of grievances of the aggrieved person by taking into account the measures or remedies suggested by the parties for counseling and reformulating the terms for the settlement, wherever

required.

(10) The Counsellor shall not be bound by the provisions of the Indian Evidence Act, 1872 or the Code of Civil Procedure, 1908, or the Code of Criminal Procedure, 1973, and his action shall be guided by the principles of fairness and justice and aimed at finding way to bring an end to domestic violence to the satisfaction of the aggrieved person and in making such an effort the Counsellor shall give due regard to the wishes and sensibilities of the aggrieved person.

(11) The Counsellor shall submit his report to the Magistrate as expeditiously as possible for appropriate action.

(12) In the event the Counsellor arrives at a resolution of the dispute, he shall record the terms of settlement and get the same endorsed by the parties.

(13) The court may, on being satisfied about the efficacy of the solution and after making a preliminary enquiry from the parties and after, recording reasons for such satisfaction, which may include undertaking by the respondents to refrain from repeating acts of domestic violence, admitted to have been committed by the respondents, accept the terms with or without conditions.

(14) The court shall, on being so satisfied with the report of counselling, pass an order, recording the terms of the settlement or an order modifying the terms of the settlement on being so requested by the aggrieved person, with the consent of the parties.

(15) In cases, where a settlement cannot be arrived at in the counselling proceedings, the Counsellor shall report the failure of such proceedings to the Court and the court shall proceed with the case in accordance with the provisions of the Act.

(16) The record of proceedings shall not be deemed to be material on record in the case on the basis of which any inference may be drawn or an order may be passed solely based on it.

(17) The Court shall pass an order under section 25, only after being satisfied that the application for such an order is not vitiated by force, fraud or coercion or any other factor and the reasons for such satisfaction shall be recorded in writing in the order, which may include any undertaking or surety given by the respondent.

High Court of Calcutta in **Puspendu Biswas vs.The State of West Bengal and Ors. 2015(1)CLJ(CAL)212** has observed on the importance of counselling in matrimonial disputes as under;

"9. The whole idea behind appointment of counsellors and securing the service of welfare expert is nothing but an endeavour to settle the dispute amicably. For change of mind of the parties who may be at loggerheads, there is need of counselling. The word "Counsel" means "advice and assistance given by one person to another in regard to a legal matter, proposed line of conduct, or contention (vide Blacks' Law Dictionary, 6th Edition). The stage of counselling arises when the Magistrate is in seisin of an application under Section 12 of the Act and the Magistrate may "direct the respondent or the aggrieved person, either singly or jointly to undergo counselling with any member of a service provider who possesses such qualifications and experience in counselling as may be prescribed."

"Sub-rule (9) of Rule 14 specifically provides that "the Counsellor shall strive to arrive at a settlement of the dispute by suggesting measures for redressal of grievances of the aggrieved person by taking into account the measures or remedies suggested by the parties for counselling and reformulating the terms for the settlement, wherever required."

10. Thus, it becomes clear as day that a Court dealing with matrimonial disputes is under statutory obligation to make endeavour for amicable settlement of the dispute between the parties through counselling/mediation. In this context, it should be mentioned here that the Act cannot be said to be a penal statute. The power under the Act can be exercised even by a Civil Court or a Family Court. In the aforecited case of K. Srinivas Rao v. D.A. Deepa (Supra) the Hon'ble Supreme Court observed - "This Court has always adopted a positive approach and encouraged settlement of matrimonial disputes and discouraged their escalation." Reiterating the observation made by the Hon'ble Supreme Court in the case of "G.V. Rao v. L. H.V. Prasad reported in (2000) 3 SCC 693, Their Lordships held - "There has been an outburst of matrimonial disputes in recent times. Marriage is a sacred ceremony, the main purpose of which is to enable a young couple to settle down in life and live peacefully. But little matrimonial skirmishes suddenly erupt which often assume serious proportions resulting in commission of heinous crimes in which elders of the family are also involved with the result that those who could have counselled and brought about rapprochement are rendered helpless on their being arrayed as accused in the criminal case. "

15. Assistance of welfare expert- In any proceeding under this Act, the Magistrate may secure the services of such person, preferably a woman, whether related to the aggrieved person or not, including a person engaged in promoting family welfare as he thinks fit, for the purpose of assisting him in discharging his functions.

16. Proceedings to be held in camera: If the magistrate considers that the circumstances of the case so warrant, and if either party to the proceedings so desires, he may conduct the proceedings under this Act in Camera.

Aggrieved women are sometimes reluctant to present their woes to judicial officers in open court. Court proceedings are generally held in the open court. But the court has inherent jurisdiction to conduct proceedings in camera to do justice. Supreme Court in **Naresh Shridhar Mirajkar and Ors. vs. State of Maharashtra and Ors.; AIR1967SC1** has observed as under:

21. Having thus enunciated the universally accepted proposition in favour of open trials, it is necessary to consider whether this rule admits of any exceptions or not. Cases may occur where the requirement of the administration of justice itself may make it necessary for the court to hold trial in camera. While emphasising the importance of public trial, we cannot overlook the fact that the primary function of the Judiciary is to do justice between the parties who bring their cause before it. If a Judge trying a cause is satisfied the very purpose of finding truth in the case would be retarded, or even defeated if witnesses are required to give evidence subject to public gaze, is it or is it not open to him in exercise of his inherent power to hold the trial in camera either partly or fully ? If the primary function of the court is to do justice in causes brought before it, then on principle, it is difficult to accede to the proposition that there can be no exception to the rule that all causes must be tried in open court. If the principle that all trial before courts must be held in public was treated as inflexible and universal and it is held that it admits of no exception whatever, cases may arise where by following the principle, justice itself may be defeated. That is why we feel no hesitation in holding that the High Court has inherent jurisdiction to hold a trial in camera if the ends of justice clearly and necessarily require the adoption of such a course. It is hardly necessary to emphasize that this inherent power must be exercised with great caution and it is only if the court is satisfied beyond the doubt that the ends of justice themselves would be defeated if a case is tried in open court that it can pass an order to hold the trial in camera; but to deny the existence of such inherent power to the court would be to ignore the primary object of adjudication itself. The principle underlying the insistence on hearing causes in open court is to protect and assist fair, impartial and objective administration of justice; but if the requirement of justice itself sometimes dictates the necessity of trying the case in camera, it cannot be said that the said requirement should be sacrificed because of the principle that every trial must be held in open court. In this connection it is essential to remember that public trial of causes is a means, though important and valuable, to ensure fair administration of justice; it is a means, not an end. It is the fair administration of justice which is the end of judicial process, and so, if ever a real conflict arises between the fair administration of justice itself on the one hand, and public trial on the other, inevitably, public trial may have to be regulated or controlled in the interest of administration of justice. That, in our opinion, is the rational basis on which the conflict of this kind must be harmoniously resolved.

Section 16 of this Act specifically empowers the Magisrate to conduct in camera proceedings if facts and circumstances so warrants and either party to the proceedings so desires. Provisions of *in camera* proceeding are also found in the Family Courts Act, 1984 and Hindu Marriage Act, 1956.

17. Right to reside in a shared household: (1) Notwithstanding anything contained in any other law for the time being in force, every woman in a domestic relationship shall have right to reside in the shared household whether or not she has any right, title, or beneficial interest in the same.

(2) The aggrieved person shall not be evicted or excluded from the shared household or any part of it by the respondent save in accordance with the procedure established by law.

This Section provides that every woman in a domestic relationship has right to reside in the shared household, whether or not she has any right, title or beneficial interest in the same. Being in domestic relationship is precondition for claiming right to reside in shared household.

Section 17 (2) provides that aggrieved person can be only evicted or excluded from the shared household as per procedure established by law.

Section 17(1) has altered the notion of ownership of property to some extent in respect of shared household. A person, who has right, title or beneficial interest in the property, has right of enjoy that property in exclusiveness. Such person has complete right to exclude others from that property. But legislature, to provide effective protection of rights of women, has granted right to reside in the shared household whether she has right or title in the shared household or not. But it is pertinent to mention that

Section 17(1) provides only right to residence to the aggrieved person and not any right, title or beneficial interest in the shared household.

High Court of Delhi in **Navneet Arora vs. Surender Kaur; 213 (2014) DLT 611** has observed that this Section does not confer any title or proprietary rights in favour of the aggrieved person but merely secures right of residence.

> "*58. On the first blush it may appear quite jarring to certain quarters of the society that by enacting the Protection of Women from Domestic Violence Act, 2005 the legislature has invested a 'right of residence' in favour of wives qua premises in which they or their husband admittedly have no right, title or interest and such premises are in fact owned by the relatives of the husband.*
>
> *59. It may be highlighted that the Act does not confer any title or proprietary rights in favour of the aggrieved person as misunderstood by most, but merely secures a 'right of residence' in the 'shared household'. Section 17(2) clarifies that the aggrieved person may be evicted from the 'shared household' but only in accordance with the procedure established by law. The legislature has taken care to calibrate and balance the interests of the family members of the respondent and mitigated the rigour by expressly providing under the provision to Section 19(1) that whilst adjudicating an application preferred by the aggrieved person it would not be open to the Court to pass directions for removing a female member of the respondents family from the 'shared household'. Furthermore, in terms of Section 19(1)(f), the Court may direct the respondent to secure same level of accommodation for the aggrieved person as enjoyed by her in the 'shared household' or to pay rent for the same, if the circumstances so require.*"

The Supreme Court in **S. R. Batra vs. Taruna Batra (2007)3SCC 169** has held that under 17(1) of the Act wife can claim right to residence against house belonging to or taken on rent by the husband or the house which belongs to the joint family of which husband is a member.

> "*22. As regards Section 17(1) of the Act, in our opinion the wife is only entitled to claim a right to residence in a shared household, and a 'shared household' would only mean the house belonging to or taken*

on rent by the husband, or the house which belongs to the joint family of which the husband is a member. The property in question in the present case neither belongs to Amit Batra nor was it taken on rent by him nor is it a joint family property of which the husband Amit Batra is a member, it is the exclusive property of appellant No. 2, mother of Amit Batra. Hence it cannot be called a 'shared household'. "

The Delhi High Court in **Sumitha Didi Sandhu Vs. Sanjay Singh Sandhu; 174(2010)DLT79** has held that right to residence does not mean right to reside in a particular property.

"*48. The learned Counsel for the appellant had also referred to single Bench decisions of the Kerala High Court and the Madras High Court in the cases of S. Prabhakaran (supra) and P. Babu Venkatesh Kandayammal and Padmavathi(supra) to indicate instances of cases where the Supreme Court decision in S.R. Batra (supra) was distinguished. Those decisions are single Bench decisions and that too of other high courts and are, therefore, of no precedential values insofar as this Bench is concerned. We feel that in view of the prima facie finding that the property in question does not belong to the appellant's/plaintiff's husband nor does he have any share or interest in the same, there is no question of the said property being regarded as a "shared household" in terms of Section 2(s) of the said Act. We also find that the expression "matrimonial home" is not at all defined in the said Act and the concept of the matrimonial homes as prevailing in England by virtue of the Matrimonial Homes Act, 1967 cannot be applied in India as pointed out in S.R. Batra (supra) and B.R. Mehta (supra). There is no doubt that the appellant/plaintiff has a right of a residence whether as an independent right or as a right encapsulated in the right to maintenance under the personal law applicable to her. But that right of residence does not translate into a right to reside in a particular house. More so, because her husband does not have any right, title or interest in the said house. As noted by the Supreme Court in the case of Komalam Amma (supra) as well as in Mangat Mal (supra), the right of residence or provision for residence may be made by either giving a lumpsum in money or property in lieu thereof. In the present case, we have noted earlier in this judgment that the learned single Judge had recorded that alternative premises had been offered to the appellant/plaintiff, but she refused to accept the same and insisted on retaining the second floor of the property in question claiming it to be her 'matrimonial home.*

49. We must emphasize once again that the right of residence which a wife undoubtedly has does not mean the right to reside in a particular property. It may, of course, mean the right to reside in a commensurate property. But it can certainly not translate into a right to reside in a particular property. In order to illustrate this proposition, we may take an example of a house being allotted to a high functionary, say a Minister in the Central Cabinet and who resides in the same house along with his wife, son and daughter-in-law. It is obvious that since the daughter-in-law and son reside in the said house, which otherwise is a government accommodation allotted to the father-in-law, the same could be regarded as the house where the son and daughter-in-law live in matrimony. Can the daughter-in-law claim that she has a right to live in that particular property irrespective of the fact that the father-in-law subsequently is no longer a Minister and the property reverts entirely to the Government? Certainly not. It is only in that property in which the husband has a right, title or interest that the wife can claim residence and that, too, if no commensurate alternative is provided by the husband. "

Aggrieved woman can only claim right to reside in a shared household if she is domestic relationship with the respondent and has lived in the shared household.The Supreme Court in **Manmohan Attavar vs. Neelam Manmohan Attavar; (2017)8SCC550**has observed as under:

"*17. The facts of the present case are that the Respondent has never stayed with the Appellant in the premises in which she has been directed to be inducted. This is an admitted position even in answer to a court query by the Respondent during the course of hearing. The "domestic relationship" as defined Under Section 2 (f) of the D.V. Act refers to two persons who have lived together in a "shared household". A "shared household" has been defined Under Section 2(s) of the D.V. Act. In order for the Respondent to succeed, it was necessary that the two parties had lived in a domestic relationship in the household. However, the parties have never lived together in the property in question. It is not as if the Respondent has been subsequently excluded from the enjoyment of the property or thrown out by the Appellant in an alleged relationship which goes back 20 years. They fell apart even as per the Respondent more than 7 years ago. We may also note that till 22.2.2010 even the wife of the Appellant was alive. We may note for the purpose of record that as per the Appellant, he is a Christian and thus there could be no question of visiting any temple and marrying the Respondent by applying "kumkum", and that too when the wife of the Appellant was alive."*

The Supreme Court has held in **Kamlesh Devi Vs. Prabha Tyagi (Criminal Appeal 511 of 2022)** that an aggrieved person can claim right to residence even if she has not actually resided against whom the allegations have been made.

"It is held that it is not mandatory for the aggrieved person, when she is related by consanguinity, marriage or through a relationship in the nature of marriage, adoption or are family members living together as a joint family, to actually reside with those persons against whom the allegations have been levelled at the time of commission of domestic violence. If a woman has the right to reside in the shared household under Section 17 of the D.V. Act and such a woman becomes an aggrieved person or victim of domestic violence, she can seek reliefs under the provisions of D.V. Act including enforcement of her right to live in a shared household"

18. Protection orders- The Magistrate, may, after giving the aggrieved person and the respondent an opportunity of being heard and on being prima facie satisfied that domestic violence has taken place or is likely to take place, pass a protection order in favour of the aggrieved person and prohibit the Respondent from-
   (a) committing any act of domestic violence;
   (b) aiding or abetting in the commission of acts of domestic violence;
   (c) entering the place of employment of the aggrieved person or , if the person aggrieved is a child , its school or any other place frequented by the aggrieved person;

(d) attempting to communicate in any form, whatsoever, with the aggrieved person , including personal, oral or written or electronic or telephonic contact;

(e) alienating any assets , operating bank lockers or bank accounts used to held or enjoyed by both the parties , jointly by the aggrieved person and the respondent or singly by he respondent, including her stridhan or any other property held either jointly by the parties or separately by them without the leave of the Magistrate;

(f) causing violence to the dependents, other relatives or any person who give the aggrieved person assistance from domestic violence.

(g) committing any other act as specified in the protection order.

The first requirement of victim of domestic violence is protection from further incidents of domestic violence. Such protection is required not only for the aggrieved person but also for her children, dependents and relatives.

Magistrate is empowered to pass various kinds of protection orders against the Respondents under Section 18 of the Act. Before passing protection orders, the magistrate has to grant opportunity of being heard to the aggrieved person as well as the respondent. After hearing both the parties if the magistrate is prima facie satisfied that domestic violence has taken place or likely to take place, the magistrate can pass protection orders.

Protection orders are preventive and protective in nature. The power of the magistrate to pass protection orders are vast and same depends on the facts and circumstances of the case and reliefs prayed by the aggrieved person in the application under Section 12 of the Act. Magistrate can pass following kind of protection orders:

- Prohibiting acts of domestic violence by granting an injunction against the Respondents from repeating any act of domestic violence
- Prohibiting the respondent(s) from entering the school/college/ workplace
- Prohibiting the aggrieved person from going to her school
- Prohibiting any form of communication by the Respondent with the aggrieved person
- Prohibiting alienation of assets by the Respondent
- Prohibiting operation of joint ban lockers/accounts by the Respondent and allowing the aggrieved person to operate the same
- Directing the respondents to stay away from the dependents/relatives/ any other person of the aggrieved person to prohibit violence against

them

The list is inclusive and the magistrate can pass other relevant protection orders based on unique facts and circumstances of the case.

19. Residence orders: (1) While disposing of an application under sub-section (1) of section 12, the Magistrate may on being satisfied that domestic violence has taken place, pass a residence order-

(a) restraining the respondent from dispossessing or in any other manner disturbing the possession of the aggrieved person from the shared household, whether or not the respondent has a legal or equitable interest in the shared household;

(b) directing the respondent to remove himself from the shared household;

(c) restraining the respondent or any of his relatives from entering any portion of the shared household in which the aggrieved person resides;

(d) restraining the respondent from alienating or disposing off the shared household or encumbering the same;

(e) restraining the respondent from renouncing his rights in the shared household except with the leave of the Magistrate; or

(f) directing the respondent to secure the same level of alternate accommodation for the aggrieved person as enjoyed by her in the shared household or to pay rent for the same, if circumstances so require;

Provided that no order under clause (b) shall be passed against any person who is a woman.

(2) The Magistrate may impose any additional conditions or pass any other direction which he may deem reasonably necessary to protect or to provide for the safety of the aggrieved person or any child of such aggrieved person.

(3) The Magistrate may require from the respondent to execute a bond, with or without sureties, for preventing the commission of domestic violence.

(4) An order under sub section (3) shall be deemed to be an order under Chapter VIII of the Code of Criminal Procedure , 1973 (2 of 1974) and shall be dealt with accordingly.

(5) While passing an order under sub section (1) sub section (2) or sub section (3), the court may also pass an order directing the officer-in-charge of the nearest police station to give protection to the aggrieved person or to assist her or the person making an application on her behalf in

the implementation of the protection order.

(6) While making an order under sub-section (1), the Magistrate may impose on the respondent obligations relating to the discharge of rent and other payments, having regard to the financial needs and resources of the parties.

(7) The magistrate may direct the officer in charge of the police station in whose jurisdiction the Magistrate has been approached to assist in the implementation of the protection order.

(8) The magistrate may direct the respondent to return to the possession of the aggrieved person her stridhan or any other property or valuable security to which she is entitled to.

Domestic violence often leads to dispossession of the aggrieved person from shared household. Majority of women in India do not have economic resources and they are either dependent on parents or husband. Once the aggrieved person is thrown out of the shared household, aggrieved person has nowhere to go.

The magistrate is empowered to pass residence orders under Section 19 of the Act. The magistrate can pass residence orders of the following nature:

- Restrain the respondent from stopping the aggrieved person from residing in the shared household, whether or not the respondent has a legal or equitable interest in the shared household
- Direct the respondent to remove himself from the shared household. The magistrate can only order male respondent to remove himself from the shared household. The magistrate cannot order respondent, who is a woman, to remove herself from the shared household.
- Restrain the respondent not to disturb or interfere with aggrieved person's peaceful enjoyment of shared household, whether or not the respondent has a legal or equitable interest in the shared household
- Restrain the respondent or any of his relative from entering that portion of the household, where the aggrieved person resides
- Restrain the respondent from disposing of or alienating the shared household, wherein the aggrieved person is residing
- Restrain the respondent from renouncing his rights in the shared household without permission of the magistrate
- If the aggrieved person's residence is rented property then either to ensure payment of rent or secure any other suitable alternative accommodation which offers the aggrieved person the same security

and facility as the earlier residence

- Restrain the respondent from any loan against the house/property in which the aggrieved person is residing or to mortgage it or create any other financial liability involving the property.
- Impose on the respondent obligations relating to discharge of rent and other payments having regard to financial needs and resources of the parties
- Direct the respondent to return stridhan, or any other property or valuable security to the aggrieved person

Magistrate is empowered impose any additional conditions and pass directions for safety for the aggrieved person or any child of such aggrieved person.

The magistrate may require the respondent to execute a bond with or without sureties for preventing commission of domestic violence. Any such order is deemed to be in nature of Code of Criminal Procedure, 1973 and has to be dealt with accordingly. It is pertinent to mention that Chapter VIII of the Code of Criminal Procedure deals with security for keeping peace and for good behavior which runs from Sections 106 and 124. In these sections, it is provided that for keeping peace and maintaining good behavior, a person can be directed by a magistrate to execute a bond with or without sureties and in case of non-compliance of such order, that person can be detained into custody.

Magistrate is empowered under the Act to restore the possession of portion of shared household even after the aggrieved person has left the matrimonial home. The High Court of Rajasthan in **Rakesh vs. Rajnesh @ Manto 2012(1)RCR(Criminal)289** has held as under:

> "*6. A bare perusal of the said provision clearly reveals that while sub-clause (1) lays down the different orders which may be passed, sub-clause (2) bestows a residuary power on the court to pass any other direction which it may deem reasonably necessary to protect or to provide for the safety of the aggrieved person or any child of such aggrieved person. The said sub-clause would naturally take its colours from Sub-clause (1). This is more so, as Section 18 of the Act already deals with "protection orders", yet Sub-clause (2). also deals with the order which are reasonably, necessarily "to protect or to provide for the safety of the aggrieved person". Obviously, Section*

18 of the Act and Section 19(2) of the Act could not cover the same area. In case it is interpreted that Section 18 of the Act and Section 19(2) of the Act do cover the same area, it will produce redundancy in the Act. It is, indeed, a settled principle of rule of interpretation that an interpretation which will make a provision either otiose or redundant should be avoid. Therefore, the words "to protect or to provide for safety" would necessarily have to be interpreted as to protect and to provide safety to the aggrieved person vis-a-vis residential accommodation. Hence, the learned Magistrate has ample power to direct that the aggrieved person be given accommodation in the shared household, although the aggrieved person may have left the matrimonial home or the shared household many years ago. The intention of the laws, which are in favour of women, is to protect the socio-economic rights of women. After all, the condition of women in this country is not only precarious, but is also pitiable. In' order to protect a woman, who has been deprived of her matrimonial home and who may face certain difficulty in her material home, Sub-clause (2) gives ample power to the Magistrate to restore and to ensure that the aggrieved person has a sufficient and reasonable accommodation provided for in the shared household. Therefore, the first contention raised by the learned counsel for the petitioner is clearly unacceptable."

The Supreme Court in **Samir Vidyasagar Bhardwaj vs. Nandita Samir Bhardwaj (2017)14SCC583** has observed that the magistrate is empowered to direct the Respondent to remove himself from the shared household.

"11. Section 19(1)(b) of the Protection of Women Domestic Violence Act provides that the Court may direct the Appellant-husband to remove himself from the shared household. The order passed Under Section 19 of the Act seeks to maintain continued and undisturbed residence of the aggrieved party within the shared household and in pursuance of same it directs the Respondent to execute a bond with or without surety or secure an alternate accommodation for the aggrieved party and pay the rent for the same and restrains the Respondent from or renouncing property rights or valuable security of the aggrieved party.

12. The Family Court arrived at a finding that prima facie material was available on record to accept the allegation of the Respondent-wife on domestic violence wherein the concerned Judge had exercised his discretion Under Section 19(1)(b) of the Domestic Violence Act which provides that the Magistrate on being satisfied that domestic violence has taken place can remove the spouse from the shared household which in our opinion he has rightly done. Exercise of discretion by Family Court cannot be said to be perverse warranting interference. The High Court while declining to interfere with the order has also considered the factual and legal position."

Cielo

ALTERNATE ACCOMODATION TO AGGRIEVED PERSON

The magistrate can direct the respondent to give alternate accommodation to the aggrieved person in facts and circumstances of the case. But the respondent cannot claim as of right to give alternate accommodation to the aggrieved person. Rajasthan High Court in **Rakesh vs. Rajnesh @ Manto ; 2012(1)RCR(Civil)433** has observed as under:

"9. Lastly, the discretion of the Magistrate cannot be cribbed, cabined and confined. It cannot be argued that merely because Section 19(1)(f) of the Act empowers the Magistrate to direct the respondent to provide alternate accommodation or to pay rent for the same to the aggrieved person, the powers of the Magistrate are confined only to Section 19(1)(f) of the Act. Such as contention, if accepted, would make other sub-clauses of section 19(1) of the Act redundant."

The Supreme Court has observed in **S. R. Batra & ANR vs. Smt.Taruna Batra;(2007) 3 SCC 169** has held that order of alternative accommodation can only be made against the husband and not against the husband's in laws.

"21. Learned Counsel for the respondent Smt. Taruna Batra has relied upon Section 19(1)(f) of the Act and claimed that she should be given an alternative accommodation. In our opinion, the claim for alternative accommodation can only be made against the husband and not against the husband's in-laws or other relatives."

Delhi High Court in ***Ajay Kumar Jain vs. Baljit Kaur Jain 160(2009)DLT401*** has held that wife can not have a right to particular property and can be provided alternate accommodation.

> "*10. Learned Single Judge in the impugned order has laid great emphasis on the fact that both the appellant and the respondent had been originally residing in the suit property being the first floor. We, however, feel that a matrimonial home is a place where both the parties seek to reside and the object of protecting the same is that the wife should not be left homeless by any action of the husband. We are in agreement with the submission of learned Counsel for the appellant that the wife cannot have a right of living in a particular property and the same cannot become a clog on the property denying the right of the appellant to deal with the property when he is willing to provide an alternative matrimonial home. It has to be appreciated that the claim of the respondent is not to any title, but of residence in the home. The appellant and his brother seek separation. The brother of the appellant cannot be denied his right to realize the best value for his share of the property or get enjoyment of a demarcated share. The brother of the appellant owes no obligation to the respondent. We are, thus, unable to agree with the conclusion of learned Single Judge that there should be a blanket injunction against the appellant restraining him from alienating or selling the suit property other than partitioning it by way of metes and bounds. In fact, there is no merit in the cross-objections in this behalf of the respondent.*"*

20. Monetary reliefs: (1) While disposing of an application under sub section (1) of section 12, the Magistrate may direct the respondent to pay monetary relief to meet the expenses incurred and losses suffered by the aggrieved person and any child of the aggrieved person as a result of the domestic violence and such relief may include, but not limited to -

(a) the loss of earning;

(b) the medical expenses;

(c)the loss caused due to the destruction, damage or removal of any property from the control of the aggrieved person; and

(d) the maintenance of the aggrieved person as well as her children, if any, including an order under or in addition to an order or maintenance under section 125 of the Code of Criminal Procedure, 1973 (2 of 1974) or

any other law for time being in force.

(2) The monetary relief granted under this section shall be adequate, fair and reasonable and consistent with the standard of living to which the aggrieved person is accustomed.

(3) The Magistrate shall have the power to order an appropriate lump sump payment or monthly payment of maintenance , as the nature and circumstances of the case may require,

(4)The Magistrate shall send a copy of the order of monetary relief made under sub-section (1) to the parties to the application and to the in charge of the police station within the local limits of whose jurisdiction the respondent resides.

(5) The respondent shall pay the monetary relief granted to the aggrieved person within the period specified in the order under sub-section (1).

(6) Upon the failure of the Respondent to make payment in terms of the order under sub-section (1), the Magistrate may direct the employer or a debtor of the Respondent, to directly pay to the aggrieved person or to deposit with the court a portion of the wages or salaries or debt due to or accrued to the credit of the Respondent , which amount may be adjusted towards the monetary relief payable by the Respondent.

Majority of women are dependent economically on husband or parents. Once a victim of domestic violence stops getting financial support from perpetrators of domestic violence her survival is at stake, as she needs money for day to day expenses and maintenance for herself and her children.

Section 20 provided monetary reliefs to the aggrieved person. The scope of monetary relief under Section 20 of this Act is much wider in comparison to Section 125 of the Code of Criminal Procedure. Section 125 of the Code of Criminal Procedure only provides for maintenance but Section 20 of the Protection of Women from Domestic Violence Act, 2005 provides for monetary relief against loss of earning, medical expenses, destruction, damage and removal of any property.

The magistrate under Section 20 has wide powers to grant monetary relief to the aggrieved person and this power is inclusive in nature. Monetary reliefs can be granted to the aggrieved person for the following:

- Monetary relief for the loss of earning
- Monetary relief for the medical expenses

- Monetary relief for loss caused due to destruction, damage, or removal of any property from the control of the aggrieved person;
- Monetary relief for maintenance for the aggrieved person as well as her children

The magistrate has to order a copy of order for monetary relief to be sent to the parties to the application and to the officer in charge of the police station.

If the respondent does not pay as per the order of the magistrate, the magistrate can direct the employer or the debtor of the respondent to pay directly to the aggrieved person a part of wages or salary or debt. Alternatively the magistrate can also direct the employer or the debtor of the respondent to deposit a part of the wages or salary or debt with the court. The said amount may be adjusted against the order of monetary relief.

MAINTENANCE TO THE AGGRIEVED PERSON

Provision of maintenance to woman and children are available under various legislations. Section 125 of the Code of Criminal Procedure, 1973 provides for maintenance *interalia* to wives and children. Section 24 of the Hindu Marriage Act also provides for maintenance to wife in suits *pendent lite*.

The magistrate has been empowered under Section 20 of the Act to grant maintenance to aggrieved person and her children. The reliefs available under this Act are in addition to other remedies available to the aggrieved person. Thus the aggrieved person can seek maintenance under this section even if she has filed application under section 125 of code of civil procedure, 1973 or any other law.

The magistrate can order for lump sum payment of maintenance or monthly payment of maintenance as per nature and circumstances of the matter.

Aggrieved person need not establish her case in terms of Section 125 of Code of Criminal Procedure, 1973. High Court of Chhattishgarh has held in **Rajesh Kurre vs. Safurabai and Ors. 2009(1)MPHT37(CG)** as under:

> "*12. The golden rule of interpretation of statutes is that the words of a statute must prima facie be given their ordinary meaning. The*

words of provisions under Section 20 of the Act are clear, plain and unambiguous. The provisions are independent and are in addition to any other remedy available to the aggrieved under any legal proceeding before the Civil Court, Criminal Court or Family Court. The provisions are not dependent upon Section 125 of the Code or any other provisions of the Family Courts Act, 1984 or any other Act relating to award of maintenance. In case of award of maintenance to the aggrieved person under the provisions of the Act, the Court is competent to award maintenance to the aggrieved person and child of the aggrieved person in accordance with the provisions of Section 20 of the Act and the aggrieved person is not required to establish his case in terms of Section 125 of the Code. Learned Trial Court after arriving at a finding that the non-applicants are aggrieved as a result of domestic violence has awarded maintenance in accordance with Section 20 of the Act. The Trial Court has committed neither any illegality nor any infirmity while passing the order impugned."

In ***Juveria Abdul Majid Patni Vs. Atif Iqbal Mansoori (2014) 10SCC736*** the Supreme Court has observed as under:

"*The monetary reliefs as stipulated under Section 20 is different from maintenance, which can be in addition to an order of maintenance under section 125 of Code of Criminal Procedure or any other law. Such monetary relief can be granted to meet the expenses incurred and losses suffered by the aggrieved person and child of the aggrieved person as a result of domestic violence, which is not dependent on the question whether the aggrieved person, on the date of filing of the the application under section 12 is in a domestic relationship with the respondent.*"

Cielo

MAINTENANCE TO BE ADEQUATE, FAIR AND REASONABLE

Maintenance granted to the aggrieved person and her children cannot be bare minimum. The Supreme Court has consistently held that maintenance has to be consistent with the status of family in context of maintenance under Section 125 of Code of Criminal Procedure, 1973.

In ***Jasbir Kaur Sehgal vs. District Judge, Dehradun and Ors. (1997)7SCC7***, the Supreme Court has held that amount of maintenance should be such as she can live in reasonable comfort considering her status and the mode of life- she was used to when she lived with her husband

> *"8. Wife has no fixed abode of residence she says, she is living in Gurudwara with her eldest daughter for safety. On the other hand husband has sufficient income and a house to him. Wife has not claimed any litigation expenses in this appeal. She is aggrieved only because of the paltry amount of maintenance fixed by the Courts. No set formula can be laid for fixing the amount of maintenance. It has, in very nature of things, to depend on the facts and circumstances of each case. Some scope for leverage can, however, be always there. Court has to consider the status of the parties, their respective needs, capacity of the husband to pay having regard to his reasonable expenses for his own maintenance and those he is obliged under the law and statutory but involuntary payments or deductions. Amount of maintenance fixed for the wife should be such as she can live in reasonable comfort considering her status and the mode of life- she was used to when she lived with her husband and also that she does not feel handicapped in the prosecution of her case. At the same time, the amount so fixed cannot be excessive or extortionate. In the circumstances of the present case we fix maintenance pendente lite at the rate of Rs. 5,000/- per month payable by respondent-husband to the appellant-wife."*

The Supreme Court in ***Chaturbhuj vs. Sita Bai (2008)2SCC316*** has observed that amount of maintenance should be neither luxurious nor penurious but what is consistent with status of a family.

> *"8. In an illustrative case where wife was surviving by begging, would not amount to her ability to maintain herself. It can also be not said that the wife has been capable of earning but she was not making an effort to earn. Whether the deserted wife was unable to maintain herself, has to be decided on the basis of the material placed on record. Where the personal income of the wife is insufficient she can claim maintenance under Section 125 Cr.P.C. The test is whether the wife is in a position to maintain herself in the way she was*

used to in the place of her husband. In Bhagwan v. Kamla Devi 1975CriLJ40 it was observed that the wife should be in a position to maintain standard of living which is neither luxurious nor penurious but what is consistent with status of a family. The expression "unable to maintain herself" does not mean that the wife must be absolutely destitute before she can apply for maintenance under Section 125 Cr.P.C."

It has been specifically included under this Act that monetary relief granted under this section shall be adequate, fair and reasonable and consistent with the standard of living to which the aggrieved person is accustomed. In **P.K. Nagrajan vs. N. Jeyrani;Crl.R.C.(MD).No.570 of 2013** the Madras High Court has observed as under:

"*16.Section 20(2)of the Act casts a duty upon the Court to award a fair, adequate and reasonable maintenance while keeping in mind the standard of living to which the aggrieved person has used to. In the present case since the respondent wife had lived in the USA, naturally she was used to a high standard of living. Therefore, the maintenance of $ 2000 per month is most fair, and reasonable.*"

Cielo

LIABILITY TO PAY MAINTENANCE NOT LIMITED TO HUSBAND ONLY

High Court of Madhya Pradesh in **Ramu Singh Tomar and Ors. vs. Bhuri Bai and Ors. III(2017)DMC581MP** has held that use of word 'respondent' cannot be given restricted meaning in Section 20.

"*32. Thus, it is clear that monetary relief is different from maintenance, therefore, it cannot be said that in view of Section 20(1)(d) of The Act, 2005 merely because it has been mentioned that the monetary relief would not be limited to maintenance under Section 125 of Cr.P.C. or any other law for the time being in force, therefore, the monetary relief on monthly basis should be treated as personal obligation of husband. In fact monetary relief is awarded to an aggrieved person to meet expenses incurred and losses suffered by her as a result of the domestic violence. Therefore, the use of word "respondent" in Section 20 cannot be given restricted meaning for the purposes of grant of monetary relief on monthly basis. The submission made by the Counsel for the applicants cannot be accepted that as the context otherwise provides, therefore, a restricted meaning should be given to the word "respondent" and the word "respondent" should be restricted to "husband" only. As the word "respondent" has been used in Section 20 of The Act, 2005, therefore, it contains the same meaning which is given in Section 2(q) of The Act, 2005 and thus, the applicant No. 1 is also liable to pay monthly monetary relief, as granted by the Appellate Court."*

21. *Custody Orders*: *Notwithstanding anything contained in any other law for the time being in force , the Magistrate may, at any stage of hearing of Application for protection order or for any other relief under this Act, grant temporary custody of any child or children to the aggrieved person or the person making an application her behalf and specify, if necessary, the arrangements for visit of such child or children by the Respondent.*

Provided that if the Magistrate is of the opinion that any visit of the respondent may be harmful to the interests of the child or children, the Magistrate shall refuse to allow such visit.

The magistrate under this Act has been empowered to grant temporary custody of any child or children to the aggrieved person or to person making an application on her behalf. The magistrate can also make arrangements for visit of such child or children by the respondent. The magistrate may not grant rights to visit to the respondent if the magistrate is of the opinion that such visits can be harmful to the interests of the child or children.

The magistrate can only grant temporary custody of any child to the aggrieved woman. The magistrate cannot grant permanent custody to the aggrieved woman. For permanent custody of child, the aggrieved person has to approach appropriate forum.

WHETHER TEMPORARY CUSTODY CAN EXTEND BEYOND PROCEEDINGS

High Courts have expressed different views on whether temporary custody of child can extend beyond life of Proceedings before the magistrate.

High Court of Gujarat in *Dhaval Rajendrabhai Soni vs. Bhavini Dhavalbhai Soni and Ors.*; **(2011)3GLR1965,** has held that temporary custody order can not be equated with interim order. The custody order passed by the magistrate can be operative even beyond the conclusion of litigation before the Magistrate.

"15. Viewed from this angle, the power of the Magistrate under Section 21 of the Act, becomes crucial which empowers learned Magistrate notwithstanding anything contained in any other law for the time-being in force, to grant temporary custody of the child to the aggrieved person at any stage of hearing of the application for protection order or for any other reliefs under the Act. In essence, therefore, in any proceedings under the Act, Magistrate is empowered to grant temporary custody of the child to the aggrieved person. It can be easily appreciated that said power assumes significance when looked from angle of wife or any other woman approaching the Magistrate seeking protection against the domestic violence by husband, his family members or other relatives. A small child to a mother is extremely precious. If mother is separated from her child, her resistance is most likely to break down. It is in this regard that learned Magistrate is empowered to pass custody orders, notwithstanding anything contained in any other law for the time-being in force. Such powers of Magistrate read with Section 23 of the Act would include power to pass interim as well as ex-parte orders. It is, therefore, of great significance and importance that Magistrates while dealing with the application of an aggrieved person seeking custody of her child deal with the situation promptly and bearing in mind the objects and purpose of the Act and also bearing in mind that mother when separated from child is likely to agree to any terms and conditions, not to resist domestic violence from husband or other family members.

16. Significantly, the Legislature has, therefore, used words temporary custody and not interim custody. This is important since by virtue of Section 23 of the Act in any case, learned Magistrate has power to pass interim order which he otherwise can pass finally. Term temporary custody in Section 21 is used in juxtaposition to the term interim order used elsewhere in Section 23 of the Act. It thus becomes clear that learned Magistrate can pass an order of custody in favour of an aggrieved person by way of temporary measure not necessarily in the nature of interim order which can have life only upto life of the proceedings before him.

17. Having said so, I cannot lose sight of the fact that nowhere under the Act learned Magistrate is permitted to pass final order of custody and any order that learned Magistrate can pass must have limited validity either in terms of time or happening of an event. Learned Magistrate cannot pass order granting permanent custody of the child to the aggrieved person.

18. With above clarity, if one reverts to the facts of the case, learned Magistrate has in context of the custody provided that child will remain with the mother till the proceedings under the Guardians and Wards Act are concluded. To that extent, therefore, in my opinion, directions issued by the learned Magistrate do not suffer from lack of jurisdiction or power. "

In **Dr. Parijat Vinod Kanetkar And Ors vs. Mrs. Malika Parijat Kanetkar; 2017ALLMR(Cri)368** Bombay High Court has observed that the nature of the power is temporary and coterminous with the main application filed for protection or any other relief.

"*14. Above interpretation, in my view, receives a seal of approval in a way, when one considers the non-obstante clause contained in Section 21 of the DV Act, the purpose that it seeks to achieve and the nature of power it confers upon the Magistrate. The non-obstante clause unbounds the Magistrate from similar powers of other courts in other enactments and regardless of those powers, he can go about the issue of interim custody on his own. The purpose that this Section seeks to achieve is protection of the aggrieved person, for the time being from domestic violence, which is discernible from the condition prescribed for exercise of the interim custody power under Section 21 of the DV Act.*

Pendency or filing of an application for protection order or any other relief under the DV Act is must and in such proceeding the issue of interim custody can be raised. The reason being that it is also an issue of domestic violence as it harms the mental health of an aggrieved person who maintains a perception and is capable of demonstrating at least in a prima facie manner, that welfare of the child is being undermined. The nature of the power is temporary and coterminous with the main application filed for protection or any other relief. It begins with filing of such main application and comes to an end with disposal of the main application or may merge with the final decision rendered in the proceeding. Such being the nature and purpose of power of the Magistrate under Section 21 *of the DV Act, it would have to be said that it is separate and independent from and not covered by either of the parts of* Section 7 *of the Act, 1984. If such interpretation is not given to* Section 21, DV Act *power, the Section itself can be rendered otiose in a given case and the Magistrate will be divested of his power to adjudicate upon that species of domestic violence issue which arises from jeopardizing the welfare of the child. Such is, however, not the intention of the legislature, rather, the interpretation made earlier is in consonance with the intention of the legislature and object of the* DV Act *to protect women from domestic violence.* "

In **Sham @ Navnath Vasantrao Vs. Sau Yogita; 2015ALLMR(Cri)264** High Court of Judicature at Bombay has observed that the relief in respect of permanent arrangement for custody of child or children, which would have force even after disposal of the application for protection order or other reliefs, cannot be said to be contemplated by the Legislature, while framing Section 21 of the Act.

"*5. In order to understand the intention of the Legislature in using the phrase "at any stage of hearing of the application for protection order or for any relief under this Act", it would be useful to refer to* Sections 19 *and* 20 *of the Act relating to "Residence orders" and "Monetary reliefs" respectively, which commence with the expression, "While disposing of an application.....", the Magistrate may pass such orders. As such, the Legislature has thoughtfully and consciously used different expressions in* Sections 19 *and* 20 *on one hand and in* Section 21 *on the other. Therefore, the expression "at any stage of hearing" used in* Section 21 *cannot be interpreted to mean "While disposing of an application..." as has been used in* Sections 19 *and* 20 *of the Act. The language used in* Section 21 *is clear and unambiguous. There is no reason to take resort to purposive and liberal interpretation of the expression used in* Section 21 *to extend the "interim stage" to "final" one as has been done by the learned Additional Sessions Judge.*

16. Likewise, the expression "temporary custody" cannot be interpreted to mean "permanent custody". The aggrieved person can get permanent reliefs under Sections 18, 19 and 20 of the Act. No such permanent relief was contemplated by the Legislature in the matter of custody of children vide Section 21 of the Act. Therefore, no provision has been made for filing independent application for custody of child or children. It is only when an application for protection order or for any other relief under this Act is pending, at any stage of hearing of such application, the aggrieved person has been given right to seek temporary custody of the child or children. The relief in respect of permanent arrangement for custody of child or children, which would have force even after disposal of the application for protection order or other reliefs, cannot be said to be contemplated by the Legislature, while framing Section 21 of the Act."

Cielo
VISITATION BY HUSBAND

Husband can file application for visitation of child even if the wife has not filed any application for custody of child. In **Huidrom Ningol Maibam Ongbi Omila Devi vs. Inaobi Singh Maibam; (2011)3GLR1965** the Manipur High Court was of the view that application for visitation by husband was maintainable even if no application has been made by the wife for custody under Section 21 of this Act.

"14. As I have already indicated that Section 21 is amenable to two interpretations as is being highlighted by the parties, in such event only that interpretation which advanced the object of the provision can be accepted. It is worthwhile to note that the Act was enacted to prevent the occurrence of domestic violence in the society and keeping in view that, several protection orders including the safety of the aggrieved person and the 'child' have been contemplated to be passed. Therefore, the cause of the safety of the aggrieved person or the child is always warrants to be taken into account in interpreting the provision. In such situation, if the interpretation given on behalf

of the wife-aggrieved party is accepted, it will render the provision incomplete as in case where wife-aggrieved party seeks custody of the child, if the child is in custody of the husband and an order of custody is passed in favor of the aggrieved party, visitation right can be granted to the husband. But, if custody lies with the wife-aggrieved party, then the husband will have no remedy of visitation right if the interpretation as contemplated by the wife-aggrieved party is given effect to and thereby it can easily be said that interpretation given by the aggrieved party-wife will never advance the cause of the child.

15. On the other hand, if it is held that the husband, in absence of any application for grant of custody, can maintain his application for visitation right will advance the object of the provision as in case of child being in custody of the husband, application for custody can be filed by the wife wherein the husband can have a visitation right if order is of custody of child passed in favour of the aggrieved party. In other situation, when the custody of the child lies with the wife, there would be no occasion for the wife for filing an application for custody as it has happened in the instant case. In that situation, husband will have remedy to have visitation right by filing application to that effect. Under the circumstances, I do find that the appellate court was quite justified in holding that even in absence of application for custody being there, by the aggrieved party, application of visitation right in terms of the proviso to Rule 21 can be maintained. Thus, I do not find any merit in the Criminal Revision Petition No. 16 of 2015. Hence, it is dismissed."

22. Compensation Order: In addition to other reliefs as may be granted under this Act, the Magistrate may on an application being made by the aggrieved person, pass an order directing the Respondent to pay compensation and damages for the injuries, including mental torture and emotional distress, caused by the acts of domestic violence committed by the Respondent.

Victims of domestic violence goes through mental torture and emotional distress and need to compensated for the same. Under this Section, compensation and damages can also be granted to the aggrieved person for the injuries including mental torture and emotional distress caused by acts of domestic violence committed by the Respondent. The Supreme Court has held in *Saraswathy vs. Babu; AIR2014SC857* as under:

"15. We are of the view that the act of the Respondent-husband squarely comes within the ambit of Section 3 of the PWD Act, 2005, which defines "domestic violence" in wide term. The High Court made an apparent error in holding that the conduct of the parties prior to the coming into force PWD Act, 2005 cannot be taken into consideration while passing an order. This is a case where the Respondent-husband has not complied with the order and direction passed by the Trial Court and the Appellate Court. He also misleads the Court by giving wrong statement before the High Court in the contempt petition filed by the Appellant-wife. The Appellant-wife having being harassed since 2000 is entitled for protection orders and residence orders Under Section 18 and 19 of the PWD, Act, 2005 along with the maintenance as allowed by the Trial Court Under Section 20(d) of the PWD, Act, 2005. Apart from these reliefs, she is also entitled for compensation and damages for the injuries, including mental torture and emotional distress, caused by the acts of domestic violence committed by the Respondent-husband. Therefore, in addition to the reliefs granted by the courts below, we are of the view that the Appellant-wife should be compensated by the Respondent-husband. Hence, the Respondent is hereby directed to pay compensation and damages to the extent of Rs. 5,00,000/- in favour of the Appellant-wife."

23. Power to grant interim and ex parte orders - (1) In any proceedings before him under this Act, the Magistrate may pass such interim order as he deems just and proper.

(2) If the magistrate is satisfied that an application prima facie discloses that the respondent is committing, or has committed an act of domestic violence or that there is a likelyhood that the Respodent may commit an act of domestic violence, he may grant an ex parte order on the basis of the affidavit in such form, as may be prescribed , of the aggrieved person under section 18, Section 19, Section 20, Section 21 or as the case may be, Section 22 against the Respondent.

The magistrate under Section 23(1) is empowered to pass interim orders in any proceedings pending before him. The magistrate under Section 23 (2) can also pass *ex parte* order under Section 18, 19, Section 20, Section 21 and Section 22 of the Act.

High Court of Bobmay in *Abhijit Bhikaseth Auti vs. State of Maharashtra and Ors. ; 2009CriLJ889* while discussing on scope of Section 23(1) and (2) of the Act has observed as under:

"15. There was some debate before this Court as regards the spheres in which Sub-section (1) and Sub-section (2) of Section 23 operate. A contention was sought to be raised by the learned Counsel appearing for the 2ⁿᵈ respondent that power under Sub-section (2) is confined to granting interim reliefs under Sections 18 to 22 of the said Act and the power under Sub-section (1) is a larger power which extends to grant of any interim order as the learned Magistrate deems it just and proper which may not be covered even by any of the Sections 18 to 22. On plain reading of Section 23, the legal position appears to be different. This Court has already held that when an aggrieved person desires to claim any interim relief under Section 23 of the said Act, it is not necessary for the aggrieved person to take out a separate application for interim relief and the only requirement of law is that an affidavit in prescribed Form HI of the said Rules has to be filed by the aggrieved person. Sub-section (2) provides that when such an affidavit is filed in the prescribed form by the aggrieved person and if the application under Section 12(1) of the said Act prima facie discloses that the respondent thereto is committing or has committed an act of domestic violence or that there is a likelihood that the respondent may commit an act of domestic violence, the learned Magistrate may grant ex parte order under Sections 18, 19, 20, 21 or as the case may be under Section 22 against the respondent. Thus, Sub-section (2) of Section 23 confers a power on the Magistrate to grant an ex parte ad interim relief. The said ex parte ad interim relief can be granted in terms of reliefs under Section 18 to Section 22 of the said Act. Sub-section (1) deals with grant of an interim relief or interim order. Thus, the scheme of the Section 23 appears to be that under Sub-section (2) on the basis of an affidavit, an ex parte ad interim order without prior notice to the respondent can be passed by the learned Magistrate in terms of Sections 18, 19, 20, 21 or 22 of the said Act against the respondent. Sub-section (1) provides for passing an interim order which is to operate till the final disposal of the main application under Sub-section (1) of Section 12 or till the same is modified earlier. Though a separate application

is not necessary to be made for grant of interim relief, principles of natural justice require that before granting interim relief in terms of Sub-section (1) of Section 23, the respondent in the main application will have to be heard. Therefore, before granting interim relief under Sub-section (1) of Section 23, a notice will have to be served to the respondent. It is well settled position of law that an interim relief can be granted only in the aid of final relief which can be granted in the main proceedings. In the case of proceedings under Sub-section (1) of Section 12 of the said Act, the learned Magistrate can pass final orders covered by Sections 18, 19, 20, 21 or 22 of the said Act and therefore it is obvious that interim order which can be granted under Sub-section (1) of Section 23 can be only in terms of reliefs provided for in Sections 18 to 22 of the said Act. Under Sub-section (1) of Section 23 a relief which is not covered by any of the Sections 18 to 22 of the said Act cannot be granted. Thus in short, the power under Sub-section (2) of Section 23 is of grant of an ex parte ad interim relief in terms of Sections 18 to 22 of the said Act and the power under Sub-section (1) is of grant of interim relief pending final disposal of the main application under Section 12(1) of the said Act."

The magistrate can pass interim maintenance under Section 23 any time during pendency of proceedings. The Magistrate may grant maintenance since filing of Application under Section 12 of this Act. The Delhi High Court has observed in **Gaurav Manchanda vs. Namrata Singh; CRL. REV. P. 343/2018** as under:

"*15. I also do not find any merit in the arguments of learned counsel for the petitioner that maintenance could not have been awarded from the date prior to the date of filing of application under Section 23 of the DV Act. In the application filed under Section 12 of the DV Act, respondent has specifically stated that the petition under Section 12 is to be read with Section 19, 20 and 23 of the DV Act and she has specifically claimed maintenance from the petitioner.*

16. Section 23 of the DV Act does not provide a substantive right to parties but is a provision which empowers the trial court to pass an order granting interim maintenance in a petition filed under Section 12 of the DV Act. Merely because the trial court has not exercised the *power under <u>Section 23</u> of the DV Act, when a substantive petition under <u>Section 12</u> of DV Act was filed and chose to pass an order only when a separate application under <u>Section 23</u> of the DV Act was filed, does not mean that a Magistrate does not have the power to pass an order with effect from the date of filing of the substantive petition under <u>Section 12</u>, which in this case had also been filed read with <u>Section 23</u> of the DV Act and also claimed maintenance.*"

Cielo
EX PARTE ORDERS

The magistrate can pass *ex parte* order, if an affidavit has been filed by the aggrieved person and it prima facie shows that there is likelihood that respondent has committed an act of violence or the respondent may commit an act of domestic violence. Such *ex parte* orders can be passed by the magistrate in respect of protection orders under Section 18, residence orders under Section 19, monetary reliefs under Section 20, custody orders under Section 21 and compensation orders under Section 22. It is pertinent to mention that such *ex parte* order can only be granted by the magistrate based on the affidavit submitted by the aggrieved person.

Details of the affidavit for obtaining *ex parte* order have been given under Rule 7 of the Protection of Women from Domestic Violence Rules, 2006.

7. Affidavit for obtaining ex parte order of Magistrate: Every affidavit for obtaining ex parte order under sub-section (2) of section 23 shall be filed in Form III.

It is within the discretion of the magistrate to pass *ex parte* order under Section 23 (2) of this Act without serving notice to the respondent. *Ex parte* order can be passed based on affidavit filed by the aggrieved person. But such discretion has to be discharged in those cases where urgent orders are warranted. Such orders should be passed with due care and caution. But once notice is served on the respondent, then based on his objections, such order can be modified, altered or revoked and made absolute. The Kerala High Court has an opportunity to examine this issue in detail in ***Dr. Preceline George vs.State of Kerala; ILR2010(1)Kerala663*** wherein the Hon'ble High Court has observed as under:

"18. Though learned Counsel relying on Sub-rule (3) of Rule 12, argued that even such an ex parte order could be passed only after service of notice on the respondents and on his failure to appear and not prior to service of notice, I cannot agree with the submission. Sub-rule (3) of Rule 12 only provides that on a statement, on the date fixed for appearance of the respondent, or on a report of the person authorized to serve the notices under the Act that service has been effected, appropriate orders shall be passed by the court, on any pending application for interim relief, after hearing the complainant or the respondent, or both. That order could only be the final interim order, passed under Section 23(1) and not the ad interim order passed under Section 23(2) of the Act. It is absolutely clear from Form III, affidavit to be filed to get an interim relief under Section 23(2) of the Act. Para. 10 of Form III reads:

10. That the reliefs claimed in the accompanying application are urgent in as much as the applicant would face great financial hardship and would be forced to live under threat of repetition/ escalation of acts of domestic violence complained of in the accompanying application by the respondent(s), if the said reliefs are not granted on an ex-parte ad interim basis.

It is thus clear that an interim ex parte order in favour of the aggrieved person and against the respondents could be passed, before notice to the respondent. But even if such an ex parte ad interim order is passed, a final order under Section 23(1) is to be passed only after service of notice on the respondent. Till then it could only be an ad interim order. If the respondent fails to appear after service of notice, then a final order under Section 23(1) modifying, revoking, or altering the ad interim order could be passed, ex parte as provided under Rule 12(3). Rule 12(3) of the Rules, is to be taken as the procedure to be followed, while passing a final order under Section 23(1) and not an ad interim order to be passed under Section 23(2).

19. For the reason that a Magistrate is empowered to pass ad interim order under Section 23(2) ex parte, it cannot be said that Magistrate has to pass ex parte ad interim order granting reliefs under Sections 18, 19, 20, 21 or 22 in all cases. It is seen from several orders challenged before this Court that indiscriminate interim ex parte orders are passed under Section 23(2) of the Act compelling the parties to approach the Appellate Court, by recourse to Section 29 of the Act by way of appeal. While passing ex parte ad interim orders, Magistrates shall take the necessary care and caution. If an interim order need be passed only after service of notice, as no urgent relief without notice need be passed, there is no justification in passing an ex parte ad interim order before serving notice on the respondent. On the other hand, if an ad interim order is to be passed immediately, and any delay is prejudicial, then Sub-section (2) of Section 23 enables the Magistrate to pass an ad interim order, without notice to the respondent. Even if such ad interim order is passed without service of notice, on appearance of the respondent a final interim order is to be passed under Section 23(1) with or without modification. Even if the respondent does not appear on service of notice, the Magistrate shall pass an interim final order Section 23(1) ex parte, with or without modification of the ex parte ad interim order. If an ad interim order under Sub-section (2) of Section 23 is passed without notice to the respondents, and no opportunity is granted to the respondents after service of notice to pass the final interim relief under Section 23(1) respondents will be unnecessarily compelled to file an appeal as provided under Section 29. Even the relief provided under Sub-section (2) of Section 25 will not serve the purpose as that section would be attracted only if there is a change in the circumstances. What is to be considered while passing an order under Section 23(1) is whether the aggrieved person is entitled to an interim order either under Sections 18, 19, 20, 21 or 22. The Magistrates shall be careful while passing ad interim orders without notice under Sub-section (2) of Section 23. It is made clear that even without issuing notice to the respondent in appropriate cases, ad interim order under Sub-section (2) could be passed. But that order is to be made absolute with or without modification, after serving notice on the respondent. If the respondent does not appear, then an ex parte order as provided under Rule 12(3) is to be passed under Section 23(1). If respondent appears and objects, after hearing the respondent, appropriate order is to be passed as provided under Section 23(1). The order passed under Sub-section (2) would only be of ad interim in nature.

In the light of the earlier findings the following guidelines could be laid down to be followed by the Trial Courts dealing with the applications filed under the Act.

(i) Notice of the application filed under Section 12 of the Act shall be served as provided in Section 13, complying the procedure laid down in Rule 12 of Protection of Women from Domestic Violence Rules.

(ii) The notice is to be send in Form VII as prescribed under the Rules.

(iii) The notice to be served on the respondent shall be accompanied by copy of application filed under Sections 12 and 23 if any.

(iv) The Magistrate can pass interim order under Section 23(1) ex parte. But that ex parte order could be passed only after service of notice as provided under Rule 12(3) of the Rules.

(v) The Magistrate can pass an ex parte ad interim order without notice to the respondent, as provided under Section 23(2).

(vi) In case an ex parte ad interim order is passed without notice, or service of notice on the respondent, on his appearance, after granting an opportunity to the respondent to object the claim and on hearing the applicant and the respondent, a final interim order under Section 23(1) is to be passed with or without modification of the ad interim order.

(vii) If on service of notice, the respondent fails to appear, Magistrate is to pass a final ex parte interim order under Section 23(1) with or without modification of the ad interim order.

(viii) Magistrates shall bestow care and caution in granting ad interim ex parte order under Section 23(2). Such relief is to be granted only if urgent orders are warranted on the facts and circumstances of the case and delay would defeat the purpose or where an interim orders is absolutely necessary either to protect the aggrieved person or to prevent any domestic violence or to preserve the then existing position."

If any ex parte *interim order* has been passed, then a copy of such order has to be served to the Respondent. The Kerala High Court has observed in Dr.Preceline George (supra) as under

"13. As is clear from the statement of objects and reasons, the Protection of Women from Domestic Violence Act is enacted to provide for a remedy under the civil law, which is intended to protect

the women from being the victims of domestic violence and to prevent the occurrence of domestic violence in the society. Therefore essentially the reliefs provided under the Act are civil remedies. The penal provisions are only Section 31 and 33. Therefore service of notice on an application filed under Section 12 or interim relief under Section 23, must be in the manner provided under the Code of Civil Procedure.

14. Order V of Code of Civil Procedure provides for issue of service of summons. Sub-rule (1) provides that when a suit has been duly instituted, summons may be issued to the defendant, to appear and answer the claim and to file the written statement of his defence, within thirty days from the date of service of summons on the defendant. Sub-rule (2) provides that every summons shall be accompanied by a copy of the plaint. Under Clause (c) of Sub-rule (2) of Rule 12 of the Protection of Women from Domestic Violence Rules, for serving notice under Section 13 of the Act, the provisions of Order V of Code of Civil Procedure is made applicable. Necessarily it is to be taken that as provided under Rule 2 of Order V of Code of Criminal Procedure, along with the notice, copy of the application filed under Section 12 is also to be served on the respondent. Similarly if an interim ex parte order is passed under Section 23(2) or a notice is issued to the respondent on a petition filed under Section 23(1), along with that notice copy of the application so filed shall also be served on the respondent. Notice is to be served on the respondent, on an application filed under Section 12 or a petition filed for interim order under Section 23(1) of the Act, to enable the respondent to defend the claim so raised against him. If so interest of natural justice, apart from the provision of Rule 12 of the Rules, warrants that copy of the application shall be served on the respondent. As it is reported that there is no uniform practice followed by all the courts, all the Magistrates dealing with the application under the Act shall, hereafter sent a copy of the petition filed under Section 12 and a copy of the petition if any filed under Section 23(1) of the Act, along with the notice and interim orders, as provided under Section 13 of the Act, to be served on the respondents."

24. Court to give copies of order free of cost- The Magistrate shall, in all cases where he has passed any order under this Act, order that a copy of

such order, shall be given free of cost , to the parties to the application , the police officer in charge of Police Station in the jurisdiction of which the Magistrate has been approached , and any service provider located within the local limits of the Jurisdiction of the Court and if any service provider has registered a domestic incident report to that service provider.

Under this Section, if any order has been passed, the magistrate has to order that free copy of such order to be given to-

(i) Parties to the Application

(ii) Service provider if that Service Provider has registered Domestic Incident Report

(iii)Police officer in charge of Police Station

High Court of Kerala in **K.E. Jose vs. State of Kerala and Anr. ILR2007(2)Kerala132** has observed that the magistrate is under obligation to furnish the copies of order to the parties concerned.

"6. I do find merit in the contention of the learned Counsel for the petitioner. Section 24 of the Domestic Violence Act evidently of furnishing copies of the orders passed by the court. In the light of Section 24 of the Domestic Violence Act which is already extracted above, the burden is certainly on the learned Magistrate to ensure that the copy is furnished to the parties as well as others specified in Section 24. The learned Magistrate must certainly ensure that the copies are also prepared and are ready to be furnished to the persons concerned including the adversary in the litigation before the order is pronounced. That would be the only manner in which the mandate of Section 24 can be complied with in letter and spirit. If the mandate that the judgment of conviction and sentence must be furnished to the accused can be complied by courts scrupulously, I can find no administrative bottleneck or difficulty which can stand in the way of the courts furnishing copies of orders passed under the Domestic Violence Act as stipulated under Section 24. For the proper administration of justice, the day cannot be too far when all courts shall furnish copies of the orders in all proceedings at the time of pronouncement of the orders itself to all the parties concerned free of cost. It appears to me to be odd that the parties ordinary must await and apply for copies of all orders when it is too well

known (or can be assumed) that all parties in the proceedings would certainly be interested in obtaining copies of the order. The relic of the past and the unnecessary procedural tangles do even now compile the courts to wait for application for copies after the order is passed. I cannot imagine a situation where a party would not want or need a copy of the order. Therefore it must be the endeavour of law undoubtedly to insist that the copies of all orders are furnished free of cost atleast to the parties to the litigation as soon as (I mean simultaneously with) the order is passed. A user friendly system cannot relegate the party to make a subsequent application for copy, wait for the court to call for stamp papers, produce the stamp papers and wait uncertainly and indefinitely for the copies to be made ready and issued. The earlier we give up the anachronistic and archaic procedure and ensure that the copy is furnished to all contestants free of cost and simultaneously on pronouncement of the order, the better for the system. No further payments or procedures can or need be insisted by any system which is reasonable and humane. The development in technology must make it easily possible in the near future, if not now, for any court to hand over copies simultaneously to the litigants when the court signs the original order.

7. Be that as it may, it is only an ideal. But in the light of Section 24, there can be no doubt on the obligation of the learned Magistrate to furnish copies to the parties concerned when the orders are passed. The learned Magistrates must ensure that such copies are furnished."

25. Duration and alteration of orders- (1) A protection order made under section 18 shall be in force till the aggrieved person applied for discharge.

(2) If the Magistrate, on receipt of an application from the aggrieved person or the respondent, is satisfied that there is a change in the circumstances requiring alteration, modification or revocation of any order made under this Act, he may, for reasons to be recorded in writing such order, as he may deem appropriate.

As per Clause (1) of this Section, a protection order made under section 18 remains in force till the aggrieved person applies for discharge. Protection orders of nature as mentioned in the Section 18 of the Act can not lapse automatically. A respondent has to apply specifically for discharge.

Under clause (2) of this Section, the magistrate has been empowered to alter, modify or revoke any order passed under the act, if circumstances change. The magistrate can pass such order on the application of the aggrieved or the respondent. It is essential for the magistrate to record reasons in writing while altering, modifying or revoking the order.

Proceedings under the Act are conducted before the magistrate and the proceedings are governed by the Code of Criminal Procedure, 1973. Under the Code of Criminal Procedure, 1973 there is no provision for alteration, modification or revocation of order. Under this Act, most of remedies available are civil in nature. Order related with maintenance, residence etc. may need alteration, modification or revocation as per changing circumstances of the aggrieved or the respondent. In light of the same, provision for alteration, modification and revocation of order has been incorporated under the Act.

The High Court of Kerala in **Sheeba D/o. Jose vs. Jojan Abraham; MANU/KE/1043/2011** has held that circumstances contemplated under Section 25(2) of the Act need not necessarily be of the aggrieved person.

> *"7. It is not as if learned Magistrate, once has passed an order under Section 12 of the Act is deprived of authority to alter, modify or revoke the said order even when there is change in the circumstances. Learned Counsel for the Petitioner would contend that there is no change in the circumstances in the present case requiring modification of the order. The circumstances contemplated under Section 25(2) of the Act need not necessarily be of the aggrieved person alone as is evident from the fact that request for alteration, modification or revocation can come from the 'Respondent' as well. In other words, if there is change of circumstance so far as the first Respondent is concerned, it is open to him to move appropriate application under Section 25(2) of the Act."*

26.Relief in other suits and legal proceedings- (1) Any relief available under section 18,19,20,21 and 22 may also be sought in any legal proceedings, before a civil or family court or a criminal court, affecting the aggrieved person and the respondent whether such proceedings was initiated before or after the commencement of this Act.

(2) Any relief referred to in sub-section (1) may be sought for in addition to and along with any other relief that the aggrieved person may seek in such

suit or legal proceeding before a civil or criminal court.

(3) In case any relief has been obtained by the aggrieved person in any proceedings other than a proceedings under this Act, she shall be bound to inform the Magistrate of the grant of such relief.

The court of the judicial magistrate or the metropolitan magistrate are not only courts where reliefs under Section 18,19, 20, 21 and 22 can be sought. Under clause (1) of this Section , relief under section 18, 19, 20, 21 & 22 of this Act, can also be sought in a proceedings before a civil court, family court or criminal court. Aforesaid reliefs can be sought irrespective of the fact that any such legal proceedings have been initiated before or after the passing of the Act. Even if any proceeding was initiated before a civil court, family court or a criminal court before passing of this Act, reliefs under Section 18,19,20,21 and 22 of this Act can be sought before such courts. Reliefs under Section 18,19,20,21 and 22 can be sought only in a pending proceedings before Civil Court, Family Court or Criminal Court. An independent application under Section 12 is not maintainable before these forums. An independent Application under Section 12 can be filed only before Judicial Magistrate and Metropolitan Magistrate. Aforesaid reliefs can be sought in addition to or alongwith reliefs which an aggrieved person may seek in such suit or legal proceedings before civil and criminal court.

If an aggrieved person gets reliefs, similar to reliefs as under Section 18, 19, 20, 21 & 22 of this Act in legal proceedings instituted before any civil court, family court or criminal court, then the aggrieved person is bound to inform the same to the Magistrate.

*In Juveria Abdul Majid Patni Vs Atif Iqwal Majoori:(2014) 10SCC736*Supreme Court has observed as under:

> *"26. It is not necessary that relief available Under Sections 18, 19, 20, 21 and 22 can only be sought for in a proceeding under Domestic Violence Act, 2005. Any relief available under the aforesaid provisions may also be sought for in any legal proceeding even before a Civil Court and Family Court, apart from the Criminal Court, affecting the aggrieved person whether such proceeding was initiated before or after commencement of the Domestic Violence Act, This is apparent from Section 26 of the Domestic Violence Act, 2005. "*

In *Vaishali Abhimanyu Joshi vs. Nana Saheb Gopal Joshi; (2017)14SCC373* the Supreme Court while interpreting the scope of Section 26 of the Protection of Women from Domestic Violence Act has observed as under:

> *"36. Section 26 of the Act, 2005 has to be interpreted in a manner to effectuate the very purpose and object of the Act. Unless the determination of claim by an aggrieved person seeking any order as contemplated by Act, 2005 is expressly barred from consideration by a civil court, this Court shall be loath to read in bar in consideration of any such claim in any legal proceeding before the civil court. When the proceeding initiated by Plaintiff in the Judge, Small Causes Court alleged termination of gratuitous licence of the Appellant and prays for restraining the Appellant from using the suit flat and permit the Plaintiff to enter and use the flat, the right of residence as claimed by the Appellant is inter-connected with such determination and refusal of consideration of claim of the Appellant as raised in her counter claim shall be nothing but denying consideration of claim as contemplated by Section 26 of the Act, 2005 which shall lead to multiplicity of proceeding, which can not be the object and purpose of Act, 2005. "*

A family court can also grant relief under Sections 18, 19, 20, 21 & 22 of this Act, if any legal proceeding is pending before it. But the Family cannot entertain independent application under section 12 of this Act. The High Court of Kerala in *Raju Narayan Swamy vs. Beena M. D.; ILR2017(1)Kerala1006* has observed as under:

> *"12. Section 26 of the PWDV Act has been inserted with an objective that in addition to the provisions of Section 12, the aggrieved person is entitled to any relief available under Sections 18, 19, 20, 21 and 22 in any legal proceeding, before a Civil Court, Family Court or a Criminal Court, affecting the aggrieved person and the respondent whether such proceeding was initiated before or after the commencement of the PWDV Act. Sub-section (2) of Section 26 further envisages that any relief referred to in Sub-section (1) may be sought for in addition to and along with any other relief that the aggrieved person may seek in such suit or legal proceeding before a civil or criminal Court. Sub-section (3) obliges the aggrieved*

person to disclose the nature of the reliefs, if any, obtained in any proceeding other than a proceeding under the Act. The intention of the legislature was to enable the aggrieved person to secure the same relief in other proceedings before the Civil, Family or Criminal Court, whether it was instituted prior to or after the commencement of the PWDV Act. This would ensure to the convenience of the aggrieved person as well as the respondent and would also prevent multiplicity or proceedings and conflict of orders. However an application under Section 12 seeking various reliefs under Section 18 to 22 cannot be filed as an original or independent application before the Family Court as the Act expressly stipulates that a proceeding under Section 12 of the PWDV Act has to be filed before the Magistrate competent to entertain the application. The Family Court will have jurisdiction under the PWDV Act to grant relief to the victim of domestic violence only if there is an existing legal proceeding and the application under Section 26 of the Act seeking relief under section 18 to 22 is filed in that proceeding. The same view has been taken in Neetu Singh (supra) and Kumari Behara (supra). "

In *S vs. J; 2018VIAD(Delhi)362* the High Court of Delhi laid down principles regarding granting of reliefs by Civil Courts, Family Courts and Criminal Courts under sections 18, 19, 20, 21 & 22 of this Act. It has been held by the court that if any suit or legal proceedings are pending before civil court, criminal court or family court, an aggrieved person has option to approach such court for reliefs under Protection of Women from Domestic Violence Act, 2005. But an independent application cannot be filed before such Courts under Section 12 of the Protection of Women from Domestic Violence Act, 2005. Further, civil courts, criminal courts and family courts can formulate their own procedure for dealing applications under Sections 18, 19, 20, 21 and 22 of the Act. Relevant paras of the said Judgment is produced herein as under-

"9. Summary of principles 9.1. D.V. Act provides a remedy in civil law for the protection of victims of the domestic violence as noted in the Statement of Object and Reasons.

9.2. The aggrieved person can file the application for the reliefs under the D.V. Act to the Magistrate under Section 12 of the D.V. Act. 9.3. If any suit or other legal proceedings affecting the aggrieved

person are pending before a Civil Court, Family Court or Criminal Court, Section 26 gives an option to the aggrieved person to approach such Court for reliefs under the D.V. Act. However, no independent application is maintainable before the Civil Court or Family Court, if no proceedings are pending before them affecting the aggrieved person and the respondent.

9.4. The Civil Court, Family Court or Criminal Court dealing with the application under Sections 18 to 22 of the D.V. Act can formulate its own procedure under Section 28(2) of the D.V. Act. The word 'Court' in Section 28(2) of the D.V. Act includes Civil Court, Family Court as well as the Criminal Court.

9.5. The Court shall formulate the procedure after completion of pleadings in an application under Section 26 of the D.V. Act. 9.6. After completion of pleadings, the concerned Court shall consider whether evidence is necessary to adjudicate the application under the D.V. Act and if so, the Court shall frame the issues and record the evidence. However, if no evidence is considered necessary, the Court shall list the application for hearing."

27. Jurisdiction:(1) The court of Judicial Magistrate of the first class or the Metropolitan Magistrate, as the case may be , within the local limits of which-

(a) The person aggrieved permanently or temporarily resides or carries on business or is employed; or

(b) The respondent resides or carries on business or is employed ; or

(c) The cause of action has arisen.

Shall be competent court to grant protection order and other orders under this Act .

(2) Any order made under this Act shall be enforceable throughout India.

An aggrieved person has been conferred wider choices of jurisdictions to approach for getting reliefs under this Act. Aggrieved person can seek relief before the judicial magistrate of first class or the metropolitan magistrate,within local limits of which aggrieved person permanently or temporarily resides or carries on business or is employed. The aggrieved person can also seek relief before the judicial magistrate of first class or metropolitan magistrate, within local limits of which, the respondent resides or carries on business or employed. The aggrieved person can also seek relief before the judicial magistrate of first class or the metropolitan magistrate, within local limits of which the cause of action has arisen. Choice of jurisdiction to aggrieved person is much wider in comparison to choice of jurisdiction available to a litigant under the Code of Civil Procedure, 1909.

Vires of Section 27 of the Act was challenged before the High Court of Delhi in ***Ram Lakhan Singh vs. Union of India & Anr; 013SCCOnlineDel4844***. The Petitioner had inter alia contended that Section 27(1) of this Act regarding jurisdiction of the Courts is ultra vires Article 21 of the Constitution and not in consonance with Section 36 of this Act and Section 177 Code of Criminal Procedure, 1973. The High Court of Delhi dispelling the contention of the petitioner held as under:

"22. If we look at Section 26 of the Act, the aggrieved person is permitted to pursue other reliefs along with the reliefs provided under the Act, and it makes very clear the intention of the legislature. While looking at or interpreting each and every provision of the Act, we have to look at the intention of the legislature. In the process, we have to look at what has been said and what has not been said to be noted. In the cases of violence against women under the D.V. Act, the moment she files a complaint, she is thrown out of the house and in several cases, there is threat and there is no security to the lady at the matrimonial place and she forced to flee to safety. In such cases the victim of domestic violence finds shelter in the parents' house, in certain cases, parents won't be able to support the lady basing on several reasons and the lady is forced to live at some other place in search of employment or to pursue some course which will fetch her a job, so that she will have the financial independence. In such a scenario, if the Section specifically says that to claim "temporary residence", the lady has to stay in a particular place for a specified period, in majority of the cases, women have to prefer a complaint at the place where the husband resides, where she has no safety and protection in several cases. If the interpretation of the petitioner is taken to be correct, such interpretation would defeat the legislative intent behind the enactment of the Act and it would render the provisions nugatory. In construing the provisions of the Act, the Court has to bear in mind that it is a beneficial piece of social welfare legislation aimed at promoting and securing the wellbeing of the aggrieved persons and the Court will not adopt a narrow

interpretation which will have the effect of defeating the very object and purpose of the Act. It must be interpreted in the spirit in which the same has been enacted. The legislature in its wisdom thought it appropriate not to specify the time limit for claiming "temporary residence", in view of the practical problems that will be faced by the aggrieved person, and it is not for this Court to take up the task of interpreting the section, when the words and intention of the legislature is very much clear. We are of the considered opinion that <u>Section 27(1)</u> of the D.V. Act is not unconstitutional and the same is in consonance with the objectives and reasons for which the Act has been enacted and the provision is not contrary to the fundamental rights guaranteed under the Constitution of India and further we are of the view that a beneficial legislation is intended to achieve a much greater purpose and the very purpose of enacting such law would be frustrated if stringent rules of construction are applied. What is a "temporary residence" depends and varies from the facts and circumstances of each case and there cannot be any straight jacket formula. At the same time, we cannot lose sight of the fact that certain legislations which were enacted for the benefit of a particular sect of people are exploited or taken undue advantage of. In such cases, courts have to be very careful and see that there is no room left for exploitation."

Cielo

TEMPORARY RESIDENCE

Even the magistrate within local limits of which the aggrieved person temporary resides has been given jurisdiction. Delhi High Court in **Sharad Kumar Pandey vs. Mamta Pandey 171(2010)DLT565** has observed that temporary residence must be place of residence and this cannot be considered a place where the person has gone on a casual visit or a fleeing visit for climate change or only for purpose of contesting the case.

"*9. All legislative enactments on matrimonial disputes or custody matters make ordinary residence or residence or the place where parties lived together or the place of cause of action as a ground for invocation of jurisdiction of the Court. Domestic Violence Act is the first Act where a temporary residence of the aggrieved person has also been made a ground for invoking the jurisdiction of court. The expression 'residence' means 'to make abode' - a place for dwelling. Normally place for dwelling is made with an intention to live there for considerable time or to settle there. It is a place where a person has a home. In Webster Dictionary, the residence means to dwell for length of time. The words 'dwelling place' or abode are synonyms. A temporary residence, therefore, must be a temporary dwelling place of the person who has for the time being decided to make the place as his home. Although he may not have decided to reside there permanently or for a considerable length of time but for the time being, this must be place of her residence and this cannot be considered a place where the person has gone on a casual visit, or a fleeing visit for change of climate or simply for the purpose of filing a case against another person.*

10. I, therefore, consider that the temporary residence, as envisaged under the Act is such residence where an aggrieved person is compelled to take shelter or compelled to take job or do some business, in view of domestic violence perpetuated on her or she either been turned out of the matrimonial home or has to leave the matrimonial home. This temporary residence does not include residence in a lodge or hostel or an inn or residence at a place only for the purpose of filing a domestic violence case. This temporary residence must also be a continuing residence from the date of acquiring residence till the application under Section 12 is disposed of and it must not be a fleeing residence where a woman comes only for the purpose of contesting the case and otherwise does not reside there. "

High Court of Orissa in **Rabindra Nath Sahu and Ors. vs. Susila Sahu I (2017)DMC 653 Ori** has observed that temporary residence includes a place where the aggrieved person was compelled to reside in view of commission of domestic violence.

"12. The legislature in its wisdom has provided that jurisdiction can be invoked by an 'aggrieved person' before the competent Court on the basis of temporary residence. The word "temporarily" means lasting, existing, serving for a time only which is not permanent. A temporary residence is a temporary dwelling place of the aggrieved

person who has for the time being decided to make that place as her home. An aggrieved person who has lost her matrimonial home due to domestic violence and was not even allowed to stay at her ancestral house or at her father's place for some reason or the other and is compelled to take residence, though temporarily, either with one of her relatives or with one of her friends at a place where the domestic violence was not committed can invoke the jurisdiction of the Magistrate within whose local limits such place of temporary residence situates. The temporary residence includes a place where the aggrieved person was compelled to reside in view of commission of domestic violence. She may not have decided to reside there permanently or for a considerable length of time but for the time being. A place where the aggrieved person has gone on a casual visit, a lodge or hostel or a guest house or an inn where she stays for a short period or a residence at a place simply for the purpose of filing a case against another person cannot be a place which would satisfy the term "temporarily resides" as appears in section 27. The legislature has provided the aggrieved women who are financially, economically or physically abused wide options to institute a case which best suited their convenience, comfort and accessibility. Section 2(i) of 2005 Act indicates "Magistrate" means the Judicial Magistrate of the First Class, or as the case may be, the Metropolitan Magistrate, exercising jurisdiction under the Code of Criminal Procedure, 1973 (2 of 1974) in the area were the aggrieved person resides temporarily or otherwise or the respondents resides or the domestic violence is alleged to have taken place. Thus even if for a temporary period of time, an aggrieved person is residing at a place, she can seek reliefs under the 2005 Act by filing an appropriate application before the competent Court within the local limits whose jurisdiction such place situates."

High Court of Allahabad in **Vikas Rastogee vs. State of U.P. and Ors. 2014(1)ACR675** has observed that temporary residence must also be continuing residence for considerable long time but whether the temporary residence has been acquired merely for filing a case under this Act, is a mixed question of facts and law.

"5. A bare perusal of Section 27(1)(a) of the Act would reveal that the Magistrate of first class has territorial jurisdiction within the local limits of which the person aggrieved permanently or temporarily resides or carries on business or is employed. Temporary residence of aggrieved person makes it possible to initiate proceedings under the D.V. Act from that place. Ordinarily question of 'residence' is a mixed question of facts and law, therefore, it has to be decided keeping in mind the facts and circumstances of each case. It is true that the temporary residence ordinarily does not include the residence in hotel or hostel or places of such nature where the aggrieved person resides for few days or even for few months with or without any reason. These places or temporary residence of such nature cannot be used merely for the purpose of filing a domestic violence case. This temporary residence must also be continuing residence for considerable long time but whether the temporary residence has been acquired merely for filing a case under the D.V. Act, is a mixed question of facts and law, and it cannot be decided by the revisional Court. It can only be decided by trial Court after recording evidence."

28. Procedure- (1) Save as otherwise provided in this Act, all proceedings under sections 12, 18, 19,20, 21, 22, 23 and offences under section 31 shall be governed by the provisions of the Code of Criminal Procedure, 1973 (2 of 1974).

(2) Nothing in sub-section (1) shall prevent the court from laying down its own procedure for disposal of an application under section 12 or under sub-section (2) of section 23.

Most of remedies available under the Act are civil in nature. But Section 28 of this Act provides that Proceedings under Section 12, 18, 19, 20, 21, 22, 23 and 31 shall be governed by the provisions of the Code of Criminal Procedure, 1973.

Although, Section 28 (1) states that proceedings under sections 12, 18, 19, 20, 21, 22, 23 & 31 are governed by the provisions of the Code of Criminal Procedure, The magistrate is not bound to follow the same strictly in light of Section 28 (2) of the Act. Section 28(2) empowers the magistrate to lay down it own procedure for disposal of an application under section 12 or under subsection 2 of Section 23.

High Court of Patna has observed in **Manish Kumar Soni and Ors vs. The State of Bihar; 2016(4)Crimes236(Pat.)** as under:

"25. All the above remedies envisaged in Sections 17 to 22 are basically civil reliefs. There are only two penal provisions in the Act i.e., Section 31 which stipulates penalty for breach of protection order by respondent and Section 33 which stipulates penalty for not discharging duty by Protection Officer.

26. Hence, a Magistrate is not required to proceed when an application is filed under Section 12 of the Act like a regular complaint under Section 200 or 202 of the Cr.P.C. Though in the present case, the Magistrate has proceeded on the application under Section 12 of the Act like a regular complaint but the same has in no way, prejudiced the petitioners.

27. Hence, though the provision under Section 28(1) of the Act stipulates that the proceeding under Section 12 of the Act shall be governed by the provisions of the Code of Criminal Procedure, but the same is directory in nature and any departure from the provisions of Code of Criminal Procedure will not vitiate the proceeding initiated under Section 12 of the Act.

28. It has been held in the case of Naorem Shamungou Singh vs. Moirangthem Guni Devi, reported in AIR 2014 Manipur 25, that in view of Sub-Section 2 of Section 23 of the Act, the Court can devise its own procedure for disposal of an application in proceedings under Section 12 of he Act and that it is not incumbent upon the Magistrate or the Court concerned to strictly adhere to the provisions of Cr.P.C. and a departure could accordingly be made from the provisions of Cr.P.C., if need arises and a method, which is just and fair, could be adopted. So far as Rule 6(5) of the Rules is concerned, which provides that applications under Section 12 of the Act shall be dealt and orders enforced in the manner laid down in Section 125 of the Cr.P.C. 1973, it has been held that Section 126 of the Cr.P.C. which governs the proceeding under Section 125 of the Cr.P.C. provides for ex-parte proceedings if the Magistrate is satisfied that the person concerned is avoiding attendance of the Court and thus the same also applies to a proceeding under the Act, 2006, when the petitioners, in spite of proper service of notice and being fully aware of the proceedings before the Magistrate chose not to appear before the Court."

Cielo

POWER TO LAY DOWN OWN PROCEDURE

The Court has been empowered to lay down its own procedure under Section 23 (2) of this Act for disposal of Application under Section 12 or under sub-section (2) of Section 23, but such procedure has to confirm to basic principles of judicial procedure. Such procedure cannot be arbitrary.

In ***Nirmal Jeet Kaur vs. State of Uttarakhand; 2013 (1) Crimes 352 (Uttar.)*** The High Court of Uttarakhand has observed as under:

> "*The question, before Court, is that whether in the light of expression "its own procedure disposal of an application", can the Magistrate recall its order passed under Section 2 or not. Certainly said expression does not give the Magistrate power to pass arbitrary orders or to pass such an order which is against the known basic principles of judicial procedure. In the opinion of this Court what aforesaid expression authorities the Magistrate is that he can pass such an order which are in consonance of the basic principles of judicial procedure. It is pertinent the mention here that proceeding based on an application under Section 12, the Protection of Women from Domestic Violence Act-2005 are not the proceeding of trial of an offence. Rather such proceedings are quasi civil in nature, like the one under Section 125 of Cr.P.C. If we look in the Code of Civil Procedure 1908, we find that there is provision under rule 7 of Order IX of the Code which empowers of the Court to set aside the order directing to proceed ex-parte. Under rule 13 of Order IX of the code trial courts have powers to set aside the ex-parte decree on sufficient cause being shown by the defendant. Similarly under the Code of Criminal Procedure 1973, in respect of proceedings under Section 125 of Cr.P.C., there is proviso to Sub-section (2) of Section 126 which empowers the Magistrate to recall an ex-parte order. As such setting aside of ex parte order by the Magistrate under the Protection of Women from Domestic Violence Act-2005 cannot be said to be arbitrary or against the basic principles of judicial Procedure, particularly when Sub-section (2) of sub-Section 28 of the Act, provides that nothing in Sub-section (1) shall prevent the Court from laying down its own procedure for disposal of an application under Section 12 or Sub-section (2) of Section 23. Therefore, in the light of the above discussion this court is not inclined to interfere with*

the impugned orders passed by the Courts below. Accordingly, the petition under Section 482 Cr.P.C. is dismissed with the observation that the petitioner shall not be evicted from matrimonial house mentioned in order dated 16.02.2010, till the interim application moved by the petitioner is decided on merits by the Magistrate in pursuance of order dated 28.05.2010. It is, further observed that interim application shall be decided in the spirit contained in Sub-section (5) of Section 12 of the Act, expeditiously."

Cielo

WHETHER SECTION 28(2) CAN OVERRULE RULE 6(5)

Section 28 (2) empower the Magistrate to lay down its own procedure for disposal of an application under section 12. Rule 6(5) of the Protection of Women from Domestic Violence Rules, 2006 states that the applications under section 12 shall be dealt with and the orders enforced in the same manner laid down under section 125 of the Code of Criminal Procedure, 1973. Issues have arisen before Courts whether the Magistrate is bound to follow procedure provided under Section 125 of Code of Criminal Procedure, 1973 or the Magistrate has discretion to lay down its own procedure. High Courts have expressed different views regarding the same.

High Court of Madhya Pradesh in **Madhusudan Bhardwaj and Ors. vs. Mamta Bhardwaj 2009CriLJ3095** has taken a view that the Magistrate is required to comply with the provisions of Rule 6(5) read with Section 28(1) of this Act and is required to follow the procedure as laid down in the Code of Criminal Procedure, 1973 for the application under Section 125 of Cr.P.C.

"8-A. It is true that nowhere in the Act any direction with regard to receiving or recording of evidence of the parties has specifically been mentioned. While inserting the provision with regard to procedure, Sub-section (1) of Section 28 of the Act a general and wide mandate has been given that all the proceedings under Sections 12, 18, 19, 20, 21, 22 and 23 of the Act (including Section 12 of the Act also) shall be governed by the provisions of Code of Criminal Procedure, 1973. The word 'shall' gives a mandate that the procedure as laid down in Cr.P.C. shall have to be followed. It is also true that in Cr.P.C. for various type of cases different procedures have been mentioned e.g. in; (1) Chapter VIII, which deals with security for keeping the

peace and for good behaviour, (2) Chapter IX, which deals with order for maintenance of wives, children and parents, (3) Chapter X, which deals with maintenance of public order and tranquility, and (4) Chapter XVIII to Chapter XXIX, which provide different procedures for trial of different offences. But, at the same time the Legislature in its wisdom has inserted Section 37 in the Act vesting powers with the Central Government to make Rules for carrying out different provisions of the Act. Sub-section (2) of Section 37 indicates that the Rule making power of the Central Government is very wide, in which it is provided that- in particular and without prejudice to the generality of the foregoing powers, such Rules may provide for all or any of the following matters, namely, (a) to (m).

8-B. Thus, although in Clause (a) to (I) some subjects have been enumerated on which the Rules may be framed by the Central Government, but at the same time it is also mentioned that this illustration of the subjects will not prejudice the generality of the powers given to the Central Government for framing Rules to carry out the provisions of the Act. This intention of the Legislature is further visible by perusing Clause (m) which provides that- rules may be framed on any other matter which has to be, or may be, prescribed. Under Section 37 of the Act, the Rules are framed which have been published in the Gazette of India. Extra., Pt.II, Section 3(i), dated 17th October, 2006, vide G.S.R No. 644(E), dated 17th October, 2006. Thus, these Rules framed by the Central Government are having statutory force and shall require to be given effect to. Although vide Sub-section (3) of Section 37 of the Act the parliament can amend or disagree with the Rules, yet unless such amendment or disagreement comes in existence, the operation of these Rules will remain in force and have to be effective. Perhaps considering the ambiguous situation, that in Section 28(1) of the Act the Legislature has given a mandate to follow the procedure as laid down in Cr.P.C., but the same has not been clarified as to what procedure will be adopted in dealing with the application under Section 12 of the Act, the Rule 6(5) has been framed. It appears that now the ambiguity has been removed by Rule 6(5) in further mandatory words by mentioning, that- the application under Section 12 shall be dealt with and order enforced in the same manner as laid down under Section 125 of Cr.P.C.

8-C. As observed by the three different Benches of High Court in aforementioned orders in the case of Het Ram (supra), Sankarasetty Pompanna (supra) and Pendiyala Sureshkumar Ramarao (supra) without providing opportunity of leading evidence such application cannot be disposed of. Similar is the procedure required to be adopted to deal with an application under Section 12 of the Act to comply the direction under Section 28(1) of the Act read with Rule 6(5) of the Rules.

8-D. In view of the aforementioned mandate, the learned Magistrate was required to comply with the provisions of this sub-rule read with Section 28(1) of the Act and was required to follow the procedure as laid down in the Code of Criminal Procedure for the application under Section 125 of Cr.P.C. Admittedly, that has not been followed. On this ground, the impugned order appears erroneous.

9-A. It is also true, that Sub-section (2) of Section 28 provides, that nothing in Sub-section (1) shall prevent the Court from laying down its own procedure for disposal of an application under Section 12 of the Act. By cumulative reading of Section 28 subsections (1) and (2) of the Act and Rule 6(5) of the Rules, it appears that Sub-section (2) of Section 28 of the Act appears to have been enacted looking to the peculiar nature of the Act and also the existence of aforementioned ambiguity with regard to the provision of Section 28(1) of the Act, but now that ambiguity has been removed by the Central Government under its powers given by Section 37 of the Act."

Karnatka High Court in **M/s. K. Manjunath Reddy vs. Smt. Latha A.C. Criminal Petition No. 1726 of 2016** has held that 28(2) would override Section 28(1) and 6(5) of rules.

"*2. The petitioner is the husband and the respondent is the wife. The wife has instituted proceedings under Section 12 of the Protection of Women from Domestic Violence Act, 2005 (hereinafter referred to as 'the Domestic Violence Act', for brevity). In the course of the proceedings, the court below had permitted the respondent to tender evidence by way of affidavit. The petitioner has strongly objected to the said procedure being adopted by the court below and has drawn attention to Rule 6(5) of the Protection of Women from Domestic Violence Rules, 2006 (hereinafter referred to as 'the Rules', for brevity) and has also placed reliance on several decisions of the Madras High Court, the Madhya Pradesh High Court and the Karnataka High Court as well, to contend that the procedure to be followed in a proceeding under Section 12 of the Domestic Violence Act shall be dealt with and the orders enforced in the same manner as laid down in a proceeding under Section 125 Cr.P.C. and this is evident from the express provision of Rule 6(5) of the Rules. Therefore, he contends that since the procedure prescribed under Section 125 Cr.P.C. requires that it shall be dealt with as a summons case and shall be recorded in the presence of the witnesses and the gist of the evidence shall be recorded by the Magistrate and signed by him, the question of filing an affidavit or receiving evidence by way of an affidavit, does not arise. However, Section 28(2) of the Domestic Violence Act also indicates that the procedure prescribed in respect of proceedings under Section 12 and or other sections mentioned therein shall be governed by the provisions of the Cr.P.C., 1973. In that, nothing in sub-section (1) shall prevent the court from laying down its own procedure for disposal of an application under section 12or under sub- section (2) of section 23.This would indicate that the concerned court is enabled to draw up its own procedure notwithstanding the requirement that the provisions of the Cr.P.C. would apply. This in fact would also address the requirement under the rule which application under Section 12 shall be dealt with, disposed of as in the case of proceedings under Section 125 Cr.P.C.*

3. Having regard to the object and the scope of the legislation, the prescription of such enabling provision is obviously not to cramp the style of the court which requires to address issues with some expedition. Therefore, the section providing that the court can form its own procedure, would also over-ride sub-section (1) of Section 28 to rule 6(5) of the Rules as well. "

Bombay High Court in **Aniket Subhash Tupe vs. Piyusha Aniket Tupe and Ors. 2018ALLMR(Cri)1751** has also held that Section 28(2) of the Act would override sub-section (1) of the section 28 as well Rule 6(5) of D. V. Rules.

> *"26. These principles have to be borne in mind while interpreting the provision under section 28(2) D.V. Act. As stated earlier the D.V. Act is a beneficial piece of social welfare legislation aimed at providing to the victims of domestic violence speedy reliefs, which are civil in nature. Though, unlike Negotiable Instrument Act, there is no specific provision in the D.V. Act to give evidence on affidavit, section 28(2) with words plain, simple and unambiguous gives flexibility to the Court to depart from the procedure prescribed under Section (1) of Section 28 and to devise its own procedure in deciding application under Section 12 or 23(2) of the Act. This enabling provision, which intends to achieve the object of the Act, would over-ride Sub-section (1) of section 28 the Act as well as Rule 6(5) of D.V. Rules. Having regard to the object and scope of the Act, this provision cannot be given a narrow interpretation which will have an effect of rendering it redundant, surplus or otiose. In my considered view, such approach will defeat the very object of the Act."*

29. Appeal- There shall lie an appeal to the Court of Session within thirty days form the date on which the order made by the Magistrate is served on the aggrieved or the respondent as the case may, whichever is later.

Under Section 29 of this Act, an appeal lies to the Court of Session within 30 days from the date on which order made by magistrate is served on the aggrieved person or the respondent as the case may be. Period of limitation will start running from service of order on the aggrieved or the respondent.

MAINTAINABLITY OF APPEAL AGAINST INTERIM ORDER & EX PARTE ORDER

Section 29 does not specify whether the term "order" in under Section 29 will include interim order and *ex parte* order. Majority of High Courts are of view that Appeal under Section 29 is maintainable both against final order, interim order and *ex parte* order.

In **Mr. G. Balasubramanian vs. Mrs. Jayashree Rajagopalan, (Criminal Original Petition No. 15455 of 2008)** Madras High Court has held that a plain reading of <u>Section 29</u> of the Act does not make any distinction between the final order and the interim order and therefore an appeal will lie both against the final order and an interim order passed by the magistrate.

"5. I am unable to accept the said contention of the learned senior counsel for the petitioners. A reading of <u>Section 29</u> of the Act does not show that the right of appeal is restricted only in respect of a final order passed by the learned Sessions Judge and nowhere in the Act it is stated that an appeal will not lie against any interim order passed by the learned Magistrate. A plain reading of <u>Section 29</u> of the Act does not make any distinction between the final order and the interim order and therefore in the considered view of this Court an appeal will lie both against the final order and an interim order passed by the learned Magistrate in the exercise of powers conferred on him under this Act. Therefore this Court is of the considered view that the preliminary objection raised by the learned counsel for the respondent merits acceptance and accordingly accepted."

The High Court of **Uttarakhand in Manish Tandon vs. Richa Tandon 2009(1)UC242** has held that Section 29 connotes all types of orders whether orders granting interim maintenance orders or ex- parte interim maintenance orders.

"3. I totally and absolutely disagree with the aforesaid contention of Mr. Sharma. The word 'order' used in Section 29 connotes all types of orders passed by the Magistrates under the 2005 Act including orders granting interim maintenance under Sub-section (1) of Section 23 as well as ex-parte interim maintenance granted under Sub-section (2) of Section 23. Since the word 'order' has not been qualified by any suffix or prefix in Section 29, the clear legislative intent is that each and every type of order, irrespective of its description and nature, passed by a Magistrate has been made appealable to the court of Session Judge under Section 29. The remedy of filing an appeal under Section 29, therefore, being an alternative and equally efficacious remedy, this petition under Section 482 Code of Criminal Procedure was not at all maintainable. It was not open to the Petitioner to have bypassed the appeal forum by straightway approaching this Court under Section 482 Code of Criminal Procedure"

Bombay High Court in **Abhijit Bhikaseth Auti vs. State of Maharashtra and Ors. ; 2009CriLJ889** has held that Appeal under Section 29 is maintainable against *ex parte* order as well as interim order.

"20. Now turning to Section 29 of the said Act, it is true that an appeal will lie against every final order passed by a learned Magistrate. The question which arises is whether an appeal will lie against an ex parte ad interim order passed under Sub-section (2) and against an interim order under Sub-section (2) of Section 23. The learned Counsel appearing for the 2nd respondent relied upon the decision of the Apex Court in the case of Amarnath and Ors. v. State of Haryana and Ors. 1977CriLJ1891 . He submitted that every interim order cannot be treated as an interlocutory order. He submitted that as observed by the Apex Court there are orders which are matters of moment and which affect or adjudicate the rights of the parties or a particular aspect of the trial. He pointed out that the Apex Court has held that such orders cannot be interlocutory orders. On plain reading of Section 29 of the said Act, the orders which are made under Sub-section (1) and Sub-section (2) of Section 23 will have to be held to be an orders made by Magistrate under the provisions of the said Act. The power under Section 23 is of grant of ex parte ad interim and interim relief in terms of Sections 18 to 22 of the said Act. Therefore, the orders passed both under Sub-section (1) and Sub-section (2) will be appealable. However, the scope of interference in appeal against such ad-interim or interim orders will be naturally limited. The orders contemplated by Section 23 are discretionary orders. The Apex Court had an occasion to deal with the power of the Appellate Court and scope of appeals against interim orders which are discretionary in nature. In the case of Ramdev Food Products Pvt. Ltd. v. Arvindbhai Rambhai Patel and Ors. 2006(33)PTC281(SC) the Apex Court dealt with an appeal provided under Rule 1(r) of Order XLIII of the Code of Civil Procedure, 1908 against an interim order of injunction. Paragraph Nos. 125 and 126 of the said judgment read thus:

125. We are not oblivious that normally the appellate Court would be slow to interfere with the discretionary jurisdiction of the trial Court.

126. The grant of an interlocutory injunction is in exercise of discretionary power and hence, the appellate Courts will usually not interfere with it. However, the appellate Courts will substitute their discretion if they find that discretion has been exercised arbitrarily, capriciously, perversely, or where the Court has ignored the settled principles of law regulating the grant or refusal of interlocutory injunctions. This principle has been stated by this Court time and time again."

Hyderabad High Court in ***Jallarapu Laxman Rao and Ors. vs. Jallarapu Pedda Venkateswarlu and Ors. ; 2018 (2) ALT (Crl.) 70 (A.P.)*** has held that no revision will lie before High Court agasint interim order passed under 23 (1) and (2) of the Protection of Women from Domestic Violence Act, 2005.

"*24. The scope of appeal is wider than the scope of revision. In a revision under Sections 397 and 401 Cr.P.C., mostly the jurisdiction is limited to law whereas in an appeal, the appellate Court has got wider power of re-appreciating the entire evidence to come to an independent conclusion and reverse the orders passed by the Courts below. In a revision, unless the Court finds apparent error in the findings recorded by the Courts below shall not exercise power of revision and interfere with the orders passed by the subordinate Courts under its jurisdiction. In view of wider scope of appeal provided under Section 29 of the Act, revision against an order passed under Section 23(1) and (2) of the Act cannot be entertained keeping in view the intention of Legislature in enacting the law for the benefit of the women who are subjected to domestic violence. Therefore, any other interpretation to the provision i.e. Section 29 of the Act would frustrate the intention of the Legislature to disable the aggrieved person to redress their claim within the ambit of the provision and driving such aggrieved person may render the remedy under the Act redundant. Therefore, in view of the law laid down by the various High Courts, I am of the view that a revision under Sections 397 and 401 is not maintainable, against, either an order passed under Clause (1) or Clause (2) of Section 23 of the Act and only an appeal is maintainable against such order under Section 29 of the Act. Accordingly, the point is answered.*"

Cielo

CONDONATION OF DELAY IN FILING APPEAL

Section 29 of this Act does not bar applicability of provisions of the Limitation Act, 1963. So general law as provided in Section 5 of the

Limitation Act will be applicable for condonation of delay.

The question arose before the Karnatka High Court in *K.M. Revanasiddeshwara vs. K.M. Shylaja; ILR 2012 KARNATAKA 1614* whether Sub-section (3) of Section 29 of the Limitation Act, 1963 operates as a bar for filing the application under Section 5 of the said Act before the lower appellate court in respect of the proceedings under this Act. The Karnataka High Court was of the view that Section 29 of the Limitation Act, 1963 does not bar applicability of Section 5 of the Limitation Act, 1963.

"17. Therefore, it is clear that Sub-section (3) of Section 29 only bars the application of the provisions of the said Act in respect of any law relating to marriage and divorce. Since the matter relating to Protection of Women from Domestic Violence Act, has not been included in Sub-section (3) of the said Act, the question of provisions of the Limitation Act. not being applicable to the proceedings before the lower appellate court and the question of the application under Section 5 of the Limitation Act also not being maintainable in respect of the appeal preferred under the Domestic Violence Act therefore cannot arise.

18. The lower appellate court committed serious error in rejecting the application filed under Section 5 of the Limitation Act for condonation of delay. It is a different matter, whether the petitioner has made out a case for condonation of delay or not, but i.e., not a ground to hold that the application filed under Section 5 of the Limitation Act itself is not maintainable. Since, a reading of the provisions contained in the Domestic Violence Act does not bar the application of the provisions of the Limitation Act in respect of the appeal, the view taken by the court below cannot be sustained in law."

Cielo

POWER OF THE APPELLATE COURT TO GRANT INTERIM ORDER

This Act does not clearly provide whether the Appellate Court has power to pass any interim order. The Supreme Court in *Shalu Ojha vs. Prashant Ojha; (2017)9SCC457* did not decide the issue but made following observations:

"29. Questioning the correctness of the Magistrate's order in granting the maintenance of Rs. 2.5 lakhs per month the respondent carried the matter in appeal Under Section 29 to the Sessions Court and sought stay of the execution of the order of the Magistrate during the pendency of the appeal. Whether the Sessions Court in exercise of its jurisdiction Under Section 29 of the Act has any power to pass interim orders staying the execution of the order appealed before it is a matter to be examined in an appropriate case. We only note that there is no express grant of power conferred on the Sessions Court while such power is expressly conferred on the Magistrate under Section 23. Apart from that, the power to grant interim orders is not always inherent in every Court. Such powers are either expressly conferred or implied in certain circumstances. This Court in Super Cassettes Industries Limited v. Music Broadcast Private Limited M;(2012) 5 SCC 488, examined this question in detail. At any rate, we do not propose to decide whether the Sessions Court has the power to grant interim order such as the one sought by the Respondent herein during the pendency of his appeal, for that issue has not been argued before us.

30. We presume (we emphasize that we only presume for the purpose of this appeal) that the Sessions Court does have such power. If such a power exists then it can certainly be exercised by the Sessions Court on such terms and conditions which in the opinion of the Sessions Court are justified in the facts and circumstances of a given case. In the alternative, if the Sessions Court does not have the power to grant interim orders during the pendency of the appeal, the Sessions Court ought not to have stayed the execution of the maintenance order passed by the Magistrate. Since the Respondent did not comply with such conditional order, the Sessions Court thought it fit to dismiss the appeal. Challenging the correctness of the said dismissal, the Respondent carried the matter before the High Court invoking Section 482 of the Code of Criminal Procedure, 1973 and Article 227 of the Constitution." "

The High Court of Karnatka in **Yashaswini vs. M. Anegudde Ganesh; ILR 2016 KARNATAKA 2155** has considered this issue in detail. The Hon'ble Court has held that the session court does not have power to pass interim order except two cases i.e. (i) an order of sentence of imprisonment in a recovery proceedings under section 125 (3) of Code of Criminal Procedure, 1973 and (ii) In a proceedings under section 31 & 33 of the Act. In cases of aforesaid two provisions, the Benefits of Section 389 of the Code of Criminal Procedure will be available to the appellant. Relevant paras of the said judgment are as under:

"16. A respondent, who suffers an order of the Magistrate in a proceeding under the Act, cannot be equated to a convict under any other Penal Laws for the purpose of Section 389. However, if he is ordered for imprisonment, during the course of recovery of the monetary benefit or in a proceeding initiated under Section 31 or 33 of the Act, the order of the Magistrate which is civil in nature when prosecuted on its breach takes the complexion of an offence punishable with fine or imprisonment. Consequently such sentence becomes amenable to the jurisdiction of the appellate court under Section 389 of the Code. The J.M.F.C. Court, which passes such order of imprisonment, can as well exercise its jurisdiction under sub-section (3) of Section 389, if necessary application is moved by the aggrieved party by suspending the sentence passed by it, so as to accommodate the respondent to prosecute his statutory appeal.

17. In the absence of any express or implied provision under the Act and also in the absence of anything conferring the benefits of Section 389 automatically in respect of any or every order in a proceeding under Section 12 of the Act until the Legislature addresses this issue, the Appellate Court has no power to stay the operation of the order passed by the Magistrate with the exception of two situations noticed supra, (1) an order of sentence of imprisonment in a recovery proceeding under Section 125(3) of the Code. (2) In a proceedings under Section 31 and 33 of the Act. "

CHAPTER V

MISCELLANEOUS

This chapter covers various miscellaneous provisions under the Act including penalty for breach of protection order, cognizance of offence committed under Section 31(1), Protection of action of the protection officer taken in good faith and power of Central Government to make rules.

30.Protection Officers and members of service providers to be public servants: The Protection Officers and members of service providers, while acting or purporting to Act in pursuance of any of the Provisions of this Act or any rules or orders made there under shall be deemed to be public servants within the meaning of section 21 of the Indian Penal Code (45 of 1860).

As per Section 30 of the Act, protection officers and members of service providers are deemed as public servants within meaning of Section 21 of Indian Penal Code, while acting or purporting to act in pursuance of any of the provisions of this Act or Rules or Order made thereunder. It is pertinent to mention that public servants have been granted certain privileges under chapter X of the Indian Penal Code, 1860.

31. Penalty for breach of protection order by Respondent-

(1) A beach of protection order , or of an interim protection order by the Respondent shall be an offence under this Act and shall be punishable with imprisonment of either description for a term which may extend to one year or with fine which may extend to twenty thousand rupees or with both.

(2) The offence under sub section (1) shall as far as practicable be tried by the Magistrate who had passed the order, the breach of which has been alleged to have been caused by the accused.

(3) While framing charges under subsection (1) the Magistrate may also frame charges under section 498 A of the Indian Penal Code (45 of 1860) or any other provision of that Code or the Dowry Prohibition Act, 1961 (28 of 1961) as the case may be , if the facts disclose the commission of an offence under those provisions.

Breach of protection order or an interim protection order has been made an offence under the Act. Breach of protection order has been made punishable with imprisonment which may extend to one year or with fine which may extend to twenty thousand rupees or with both. Such offence as far as practicable has to be tried by the Magistrate, who had passed the order, which has been breached by the respondent.

The magistrate may also frame charge under section 498A or any other provision of Indian Penal Code, 1860 or the Dowry Prohibition Act, 1961, if facts disclose the commission of an offence under those provisions.

Rule 15 of the Protection of Women from Domestic Violence Act, 2005 provides procedure regarding breach of Protection Orders as under:

15. Breach of Protection Orders.--

(1) An aggrieved person may report a breach of protection order or an interim protection order to the Protection Officer.

(2) Every report referred to in sub-rule (1) shall be in writing by the informant and duly signed by her.,

(3) The Protection Officer shall forward a copy of such complaint with a copy of the protection order of which a breach is alleged to have taken place to the concerned Magistrate for appropriate orders.

(4) The aggrieved person may, if she so desires, make a complaint of breach of protection order or interim protection order directly to the Magistrate or the Police, if she so chooses.

(5) If, at any time after a protection order has been breached, the aggrieved person seeks his assistance, the protection officer shall immediately rescue her by seeking help from the local police station and assist the aggrieved person to lodge a report to the local police authorities in appropriate cases.

(6) When charges are framed under section 31 or in respect of offences under section 498A of the Indian Penal Code, 1860 (45 of 1860), or any other offence not summarily triable, the Court may separate the proceedings for such offences to be tried in the manner prescribed under Code of Criminal Procedure, 1973 (2 of 1974) and proceed to summarily try the offence of the breach of Protection Order under section 31, in accordance with the provisions of Chapter XXI of the Code of Criminal Procedure, 1973 (2 of 1974).

(7) Any resistance to the enforcement of the orders of the Court under the Act by the respondent or any other person purportedly acting on his behalf shall be deemed to be a breach of protection order or an interim protection order covered under the Act.

(8) A breach of a protection order or an interim protection order shall immediately be reported to the local police station having territorial jurisdiction and shall be dealt with as a cognizable offence as provided under sections 31 and 32.

(9) While enlarging the person on bail arrested under the Act, the Court may, by order, impose the following, conditions to protect the aggrieved person and to ensure the presence of the accused before the court, which may include-

(a) an order restraining the accused from threatening to commit or committing an act of domestic violence;

(b) an order preventing the accused from harassing, telephoning or making any contact with the aggrieved person;

(c) an order directing the accused to vacate and stay away from the residence of the aggrieved person or any place she is likely to visit;

(d) an order prohibiting the possession or use of firearm or any other dangerous weapon;

(e) an order prohibiting the consumption of alcohol or other drugs;

(f) any other order required for protection, safety and adequate relief to the aggrieved person.

As per Rule 15 in case of breach of protection order or interim protection order by the respondent, an aggrieved person can approach the protection officer or the magistrate or police. If aggrieved person approaches the protection officer, such protection officer is required to inform the magistrate in writing duly signed.

If the aggrieved person seeks assistance of the protection officer after breach of protection order or interim protection order, protection officer has to immediately rescue her by seeking help from local police authorities. The protection officer also has to help in lodging report to local police station.

Local police station shall treat the complaint regarding breach of protection order or interim protection order as cognizable offence as provided under section 31 and 32 of the Act.

TRIAL OF OFFENCES UNDER SECTION 31

Offences under Section 31 of the Act have to be summarily tried in accordance with the provisions of Chapter XXI of the Code of Criminal Procedure, 1973. If the magistrate frame charges under Section 498A or any other offence not summarily triable, the Court may separate the proceedings for such offences to be tried in manner prescribed under Code of Criminal Procedure, 1973.

CONDITIONS OF BAIL UNDER SECTION 31

Under rule 15 (9) a competent Court while enlarging the respondent on bail may impose conditions for protection, safety and adequate relief to the aggrieved person as under:

- Restraining the accused from threatening to commit or to committing an act of domestic violence;
- Preventing the accused from harassing, telephoning, or making any contact with the aggrieved person;
- Directing the accused to vacate and stay away from the residence of the aggrieved person or any place she is likely to visit
- Prohibiting the possession or use of firearm or any other dangerous weapon
- Prohibiting the consumption of alcohol or other drugs

BREACH OF THE MAINTENANCE ORDER

High Courts have taken different views regarding whether breach of protection order as provided in Section 31 of the Act will include breach of maintenance order.

The Rajasthan High Court in **Smt Kanchan vs. Vikramjeet Setia; 2013ALLMR (Cri)253** has held that Section 31 of this Act cannot be invoked for execution of maintenance order. Provisions of Section 125 of the Code of Criminal Procedure, 1973 has to be applied for execution of maintenance order.

> *"7. A perusal of Section 20 of the Act of 2005 reveals that exhaustive procedure for the execution of monetary relief has not been laid down in this Section because sub-Sections (4) and (5) of Section 20 provide the consequences to an order of monetary relief. Sub-Section (6) of Section 20 of the Act of 2005 entitles the Magistrate to direct the employer or debtor of the respondent to directly pay to the aggrieved person or to deposit with the Court a portion of wages or salaries or debt due or accrued to the creditor of the respondent towards the monetary relief payable by the respondent. However, this provision is limited to the person who may*

have accrued credit or is a salaried person, but in case of a self-employed person, this provision would be of no help to the claimant.

8. Resultantly, the Court would have to fall back-on to the procedure provided under Sec. 28 of the Act of 2005, which lays down that the Courts shall be governed by the general provisions of the Code of Criminal Procedure in relation to the proceedings under Sections 12, 18, 19, 20, 21, 22 and 23 as well as for the offence under Sec. 31 of the Act of 2005. Sub-Section (2) of Section 23 of the Act of 2005 provides for a procedure to be laid down by the Court on its own for the disposal of an application under Sec. 12 or sub-Section (2) of Section 23 of the Act of 2005. The procedure, which the learned Court below can adopt is limited to the disposal of the application, but for execution of the order, a resort has to be had to the general provisions of the Code of Criminal Procedure.

9. Resultantly, this Court is of the opinion that the provisions of the Code of Criminal Procedure in relation to execution of the order under Sec. 125 Cr.P.C. have to be resorted to by the Court below for giving force to the order of monetary relief."

High Court of Judicature at Allahabad has expressed similar opinion in **Manoj Anand vs. State of U.P & Anr; 2012ACR1500** as under:

"5. From the above it is clear that the order passed for the maintenance or interim maintenance is not included or covered by Section 18. Thus there is substance in the contention of revisionist that power under Section 31 was not available to the Magistrate to implement the order of interim maintenance passed under Section 23 of the Act and proceed to punish him for the breach thereof. Even clause (g) of Section 18 which includes, any other act as specified in Protection order would not include the order of interim maintenance.

6. Order passed under Section 23 of the Act cannot be implemented under Section 31 of the Act. The Act is punitive in nature and the provisions are to be construed strictly. In my view such act/ breach could not be made punishable which legislature did not intend, as such impugned order cannot be sustained.

7. Learned counsel for the wife, opposite party would submit that Act is a complete Code and it cannot be presumed that any order passed under the Act will be left uncomplied and there will be no provision to implement the same.

8. Provisions of the Act are to be construed in a manner so as to advance the purpose of the Act and it cannot be presumed that legislature did not intend to ensure compliance of order of interim maintenance. If this argument is accepted, Section 23 would become redundant or inoperable.

9. For this purpose power has been given in the Act itself. Section 28 of the Act provides for procedure and says that all proceedings under Sections 12, 18, 19, 20, 21 and 23 shall be governed by the provisions of Criminal Procedure Code. Sub-section (2) of Section 28 further enables the Court to lay down its own procedure for disposal of an application under sub-section (2) of Section 23 of the Act. This gives sufficient indication as to how application under Section 23 will be dealt with and how the orders passed thereon will be enforced. While Section 20 (1) (d) contains provision for maintenance. Sub-sections (4) (5) and (6) of Section 20 provide for mechanism to ensure compliance of order for maintenance. More over in exercise of power conferred by Section 37 rules have been framed for carrying out the provisions of the Act. Rule 6 (5) lays down the procedure as such it cannot be said that Section 23 being not capable of enforcement is redundant or in operable."

The High Court of Karnataka has also expressed similar view in **Mr. Francis Cyril C Cunha vs. Smt Lydia Jame D' Cunha; 2016(2) AKR 15** has concurred with view taken in Smt Kanchan Vs. Vikramjeet Setia (supra).

"14. Hon'ble High Court of Rajasthan had an opportunity to discuss the applicability of the provisions of Section 31 of the above Act in regard to the noncompliance of the order relating to the non-payment of arrears of maintenance. What is held by the Hon'ble High Court of Rajasthan is that breach of order of monetary relief will not pave way to prosecute the husband. It is made clear that section 31 of the Act does not include monetary relief.

xxxxxxxxx

15. In the present case, the provisions of Section 31 of the Act was pressed into service before the trial court essentially on the ground that arrears of the maintenance was not paid and thereforon to take a view different from the one taken by the Hon'ble High Court of

Rajasthan. As already discussed, the High Court of Rajasthan has exhaustively dealt with the scope of Section 31 of the Act in the light of Sections 2 (o), (k), 12,18, 20 and 28 of the Act. In this view of the matter, the approach of the trial court in taking cognizance of the offence under Section 31 of the Act in a glaring legal error and hence the same will have to be set aside. Consequently the revision petition will have to be allowed and the order of the JMFC passed on 28.2.2013 and affirmed in Crl. A. 211/13 will have to be set aside."

High Court of Karnatka in **Vincent Shanthakumar vs. Christina Geetha Rani and Ors.: III(2015)DMC236Kar.** has taken a contrary view and has held that breach of maintenance order is punishable under Section 31 of the Act.

"37. On plain reading of this section, the entire enactment and the provisions shall be in addition to all other laws for the time being in force which are not derogatory to the provisions of the other laws. Therefore, it goes without saying that though such remedy of recovery of the maintenance amount is there u/S. 125(3) nevertheless, Section 31 also comes to the help of the victim. It should be borne in mind that a new enactment has been enacted knowing fully well u/ S. 125 of the Cr.P.C., speedy remedy is available. Such speedy remedy is also found to be inadequate under the peculiar circumstances of certain cases, perhaps may be the reason that even an order u/S. 125 of the Cr.P.C. in some cases became futile and fruitless because of the unscrupulous husbands by using their ingenious mind successfully avoided to pay maintenance even under the enforcement proceedings u/S. 125(3), that may be the reason, that Section 31 introduced in this particular Act to make such violation of the protection order more stringent, as an offence punishable under this Section, after thorough study of all the existing laws and after taking due care and caution.

38. Having discussed the abovesaid different provisions of the Act, in view of my reasons given above, I am of the firm and considered opinion that an order granting maintenance though u/S. 23 of the Act, if it is passed ex parte or after hearing the parties to the proceedings and even after suffering that order, with knowledge of the order, if the respondent intentionally violates or abuses such an order, it shall be taken as an order deemed to have been passed to prohibit the domestic violence and to protect the victim u/S. 18 of the Act, such violation is punishable u/S. 31 of the Act, as long as such an order is enforceable, unless such order is vacated or cancelled by the competent court. "

Contrary view has been expressed by High Court of Madhya Pradesh in **Sunil (Sonu) vs. Sarita Chawla; 2010(1)MPLJ196**, where in the Court has held that even breach of maintenance order is also covered under Section 31 of the Act. The Court has held as under:

"*From perusal of the record, it is evident that the interim order passed by the learned Trial Court regarding the payment of maintenance was confirmed by the Appellate Court as the appeal was dismissed on account of delay. The interim order was not further challenged. Thus same has attained finality. Now the only question, which requires consideration is whether the interim order passed by the learned Trial Court, whereby the maintenance was awarded is a protection order and on account of breach of protection order, the proceedings can be initiated against the petitioner under Section 31 of the Act. Section 18 of the Act empowers the Court for passing a protection order against a respondent, who commits any act of domestic violence. In exercise of the powers conferred by Section 37 of the Act the Central Government, has framed the Rules. As per Rule 6 every application of the aggrieved person under Section 12 of the Act is required to be filed in Form 11. Sub-clause III of Form No. 1 deals with economic violence according to which not providing money for maintaining of food, clothes, medicine etc. is amounting to the economic violence for which the Court is empowered to pass a protection order. As per Sub-section (1) of Section 28 of the Act the proceedings are required to be governed by the provisions of Cr.PC. As per Sub-section (2) of Section 28, the Court is not prevented from laying down its own procedure for disposal of an application of Section 12 of the Act. In the facts and circumstances of the case where no amount of maintenance has been paid by the petitioner, no illegality was committed by the learned Trial Court in initiating the proceedings under Section 31 of the Act.*" "

The view in *Sunil (Sonu) vs. Sarita Chawla; 2010(1)MPLJ196* has been affirmed by larger bench of Madhya Pradesh High Court in *Surya Prakash vs. Rachna 2018ALLMR(Cri)363.*

"15. *Section 20 of the Act deals with grant of monetary relief to meet the expenses incurred and the losses suffered by aggrieved person and any child of the aggrieved person as a result of domestic violence. Such provision enlarges the scope of domestic violence as defined in Section 3 of the Act. In terms of Section 3 of the Act, the "economic abuse" includes deprivation of all or any economic or financial resources, payment of rental related to shared household and maintenance. Whereas Section 20 includes a loss of earnings, medical expenses, loss caused due to destruction, damage or removal of any property as also the maintenance. The grant of monetary relief under Section 20 does not exclude the amount of maintenance which can be awarded in terms of Section 18 of the Act as part of affirmative order in respect of the domestic violence as defined in Section 3 of the Act. Therefore, we find that non-payment of maintenance is a breach of protection order; therefore, Section 31 of the Act can be invoked. Therefore, in respect of first question, it is held that non-payment of maintenance allowance is a breach of protection order for which proceedings under Section 31 of the Act can be invoked.*"

Cielo

FAMILY COURT CAN TRY OFFENCES UNDER SECTION 31

Family court can try offences under Section 31 of this Act. Bombay High Court in **Pramodini Vijay Fernandes vs. Vijay Fernandes 2010(4)BomCR360** has held as under:

"10. *In the case of Union of India and Anr. v. Paras Laminates (P) Ltd. (1990) 4 SCC 453 at 457, it has been held that the Customs Tribunal had powers conferred expressly by the Statute and being a judicial body it had all other incidental and ancillary powers which are necessary to make the express grant of the statutory powers fully effective. The ambit of the limits of its jurisdiction is, therefore, extended to such incidental and ancillary powers as inherent in the*

Tribunal. This is on the premise that the legislative intent of the power expressly granted in an assigned field of jurisdiction must be efficaciously and meaningfully exercised. Hence it is held that though the powers of the Tribunal are limited and the area of its jurisdiction is clearly defined, but within the bounds of its jurisdiction, it has all the powers expressly and impliedly granted, implied grant being limited by the express grant. Hence all incidental powers, which would make the grant effective and would be reasonably necessary for that purpose are implicitly taken to be conferred in the Tribunal. This is upon the principle of interpretation set out in that paragraph from Maxwell on Interpretation of Statutes (11th Edition) which runs thus:

where not confer jurisdiction, impliedly also grants the power of doing all such acts, or employing such means, as are essentially necessary to its execution.

11. Similarly in the case of Shail Kumari Devi and Anr. v. Krishan Bhagwan Pathak alias Kishun B. Pathak AIR 2008 SC 2006 it is held that the Magistrate, who is vested with the jurisdiction under Section 125 of the Criminal Procedure Code for granting maintenance to wives, children and parents, is conferred the power by necessary implication to pass interim orders of maintenance. It is held that he would have such a power in the absence of any express bar or prohibition under that section.

12. Further, since the Family Court is a Civil Court and has all the powers of a Civil Court, it can pass orders consequent upon disobedience of breach of its order under Order XXXIX Rule 2A of the CPC. Further the Family Court like any other Court has the inherent power under Section 151 of the CPC to pass such orders as would be just and equitable, including orders to effectuate its own orders. In this case, the application of the Petitioner herein was specifically made under Section 31 of the DV Act.

13. The Family Court would, therefore, have the jurisdiction under Section 31(2) of the DV Act as the Magistrate which had passed the order of interim protection to frame charges under Section 32(3) of the DV Act and to levy the penalty under Section 32(1) of the DV Act for breach of its interim protection order. However, the Family Court would also have the jurisdiction to proceed under Order XXXIX Rule 2A of the CPC for breach and disobedience of its order and injunction."

32. Cognizance and proof: (1) Notwithstanding anything contained in the Code of Criminal Procedure, 1973 (2 of 1974), the offence under sub-section (1) of section 31 shall be cognizable and non-bailable.

(2) Upon the sole testimony of the aggrieved person, the court may conclude that an offence under sub-section (1) of Section 31 has been committed by the Accused.

Offence under sub-section (1) of the Section 31 is cognizable and non-bailable. Cognizable and non-bailable offence has been defined under Code of Criminal Procedure 1973.

Section 2(c) of Code of Criminal Procedure, 1973 defines the term cognizable offence as under :

2 (c) "Cognizable Offence" means an offence for which, and "Cognizable Case" means a case in which, a police officer may, in accordance with the First Schedule or under any other law for the time being in force, arrest without warrant.

Section 2 (a) of the Code of Criminal Procedure, 1973 defines the term bailable and non-bailable offence as under:

2 (a) Bailable offence means any an offence which is shown as bailable in the First Schedule, or which is made bailable by any other law for the time being in force; and "non-bailable" offence any other offence.

In *Vincent Shanthakumar vs. Christina Geetha Rani and Ors.; III(2015)DMC236Kar*, Karnatka High Court has observed on the procedure adopted for proceeding under Section 31 and 32 as under:

> *"40. On perusal of the abovesaid provision, it clears out the doubt that the offence u/S. 31 of the DV Act is made non-bailable and cognizable one. Therefore, the Magistrate has to follow the procedures as contemplated under the Cr.P.C. while taking cognizance and issuing process that means to say, the Magistrate has to apply his mind while taking cognizance u/S. 200, Cr.P.C. to the provisions of section 190(1)(A) of Cr.P.C. The Magistrate must apply his judicious mind to ascertain whether there was any breach of any protection order, interim order or any enforceable ex parte order passed under this Act in order to take cognizance of the offence under the Act and thereafter, if necessary, the Magistrate can exercise powers u/S. 202 of Cr.P.C. for the purpose of enquiring into the matter by himself or sending it for inquiry and report. It can be said that before a Magistrate takes cognizance of an offence, he must*

apply his mind for the purpose of satisfying himself with regard to the constitution of an offence u/S. 31 of the DV Act and then only he must take cognizance and proceed u/S. 202 of Cr.P.C. if he finds sufficient material to issue process, then he has to issue process u/S. 204 of Cr.P.C. An order expressing his satisfaction with regard to the existence of a prima facie case u/S. 31 of the Act to proceed against the accused is mandatory. The power u/S. 203 of Cr.P.C. to dismiss the complaint can also be exercised if the Magistrate is not satisfied with regard to the prima facie constitution of any offence u/S. 31 of the Act.

41. If the Magistrate takes cognizance and issues summons and after appearance of the accused before the court, the Magistrate has to proceed to dispose of the case in accordance with law by applying summary procedure. However, if any other provisions under the Indian Penal Code i.e. u/S. 498A, IPC is also invoked by the party or any charges are framed under the said provision, the said offences have to be tried in the manner prescribed under the Cr.P.C. The case u/S. 31 of the Act, though can be tried summarily but the Magistrate has to adopt summons or warrant trial for the purpose of disposal of the case as expeditiously as possible depending upon the other penal provisions invoked by the complainant."

33. Penalty for not discharging duty by Protection Officer: *If any protection officer fails or refuses to discharge his duties as directed by the Magistrate in the protection order without any sufficient cause, he shall be punished with imprisonment of either description for a term which may extend to one year or with fine which may extent to twenty thousand rupees or with both.*

34. *Cognizance of offence committed by Protection Officer: No prosecution or other legal proceedings shall lie against the Protection Officer unless a complaint is filed with the previous sanction of the state Government or an officer authorized by the state Govt. for the purpose.*

35. *Protection of action taken in good faith: No suit, prosecution or other legal proceedings shall lie against the Protection Officer for any damage caused or likely to be caused by anything which is in good faith done or intended to be done under this Act or any rule or order made their under.*

36. *Act not in derogation of any other law: The Provisions of this Act shall be in addition to, and not in derogation of the provisions of any other law, for the time being in force.*

The provisions of this Act are in addition to other provisions of law and not in derogation of the provisions of any other law. This Act supplements and not supplant the other remedies available to the aggrieved person. An aggrieved person can approach other forums to get relevant reliefs like filing petition under 125 Cr.P.C., approaching police station for filing complaint under Section 498A of Code of Criminal Procedure, 1973, maintenance under Section 24 of Hindu Marriage Act etc.

In *Sanjay Gulati vs. Harsh Lata ;Crl. Revision No. 783 of 2017 (O&M)*, Punjab and Haryana High Court has held that provisions of this Act are supplementary to provisions of other law.

> *"On careful examination of Section 20 of the Domestic Violence Act which allows for monetary relief, section 20 (d) provides for maintenance to the aggrieved person as well as her children, if any, which would be in addition to an order of maintenance under Section 125 of the Code of Criminal Procedure, 1973 (2 of 1974) or any other law for the time being in force. Section 26 further stipulates that any relief available under sections 18, 19, 20, 21 and 22 of the Act may also be sought in any legal proceedings before a civil court family court or a criminal court and such relief may be sought in addition to thereto. Whereas section 36 clearly stipulates "Act not in derogation of any other law.-The provisions of this Act shall be in addition to, and not in derogation of the provisions of any other law, for the time being in force." A co-joint reading of the aforesaid Sections 20, 26 and 36 would clearly establish that the provisions of the Domestic Violence Act are supplementary to provisions of other law and, therefore, this Court, respectfully disagrees with the dictum in B Prakash v. Deepa, (supra) the case as cited by the counsel for the petitioner."*

37. Power of the Central Government to make rules: (1) The Central Government may , by notification, make rules for carrying out the provisions of this Act.

(2) In Particular, and without prejudice to the generality of the foregoing power, such rules may provide for all or any of the following matters, namely;

(a) the qualifications and experience which a Protection Officer shall possess under sub-section (2) of section 8;

(b)the terms and conditions of service of the Protection Officers and other officers subordinate to him, under sub-section (3) of section (8)

(c) the form and manner in which a domestic incident report may be made under clause (b) of sub-section (1) of section 9;

(d) the form and manner in which an application for protection order may be made to the Magistrate under clause © of sub section (1) of section 9;

(e) the form in which a complaint is to be filed under clause (d) of sub-section (1) of section (9);

(f) the other duties to be performed by the Protection Officer under clause (I) of sub-section (1) of section 9;

(g)the rules regulating registration of service providers under sub-section (1) of section 10.

(h) the form in which an application under sub-section (1) of section 12 seeking reliefs under this Act may be made and the particulars which such application shall contain under sub-section (3) of that section.

(I) the means of serving notices under sub-section (1) of section 13;

(j) the form of declaration of service of notice to be made by the Protection Officer under sub-section (2) of Section 13;

(k) the qualifications and experience in counselling which a member of the service provider shall possess under sub section (1) of section 14;

(l) the form in which an affidavit may be filed by the aggrieved person under sub-section (2) of section 23;

(m) any other matter which has to be or may be, prosecuted.

(3) Every rule made under this Act shall be laid, as soon as may be after it is made , before each house of Parliament, while it is in session, for a total period of thirty days which may be comprised in one session or in two or more successive sessions, and if , before the expiry of the session immediately following the session or the successive sessions aforesaid , both houses agree in making any modification in the rule or both houses agree that the rule should not form or be of no effect, as the case may be ; so however , that any such modification or annulment shall be without prejudice to the validity of anything previously done under that rule.

Section 37 empowers the Central Government to make rules for carrying out provisions of the Act. The Central Government has made the Protection of Women from Domestic Violence Rules, 2006 under Section 37, which have come into force w.e.f 26.10.2006.

www.ingramcontent.com/pod-product-compliance
Lightning Source LLC
Chambersburg PA
CBHW070859160726
48004CB00003B/1155